THE RIGHT WAY TO CONDUCT MEETINGS, CONFERENCES AND DISCUSSIONS

In the same series

The Hon. Treasurer
Sample Social Speeches
General & Social Letter Writing

THE RIGHT WAY TO CONDUCT MEETINGS CONFERENCES AND DISCUSSIONS

H.M. TAYLOR

and

A.G. MEARS

RIGHT WAY

Printed and bound in Great Britain by Cox & Wyman Ltd., Reading, Berkshire.

The *Right Way* series is published by Elliot Right Way Books, Brighton Road, Lower Kingswood, Tadworth, Surrey, KT20 6TD, U.K. For information about our company and the other books we publish, visit our web site at www.right-way.co.uk

CONTENTS

PREFACE

The chief purpose of this book is to help the beginner who is venturing into the unknown and therefore possibly terrifying realm of procedure at meetings. It does not attempt to deal with Company Law or Parliamentary procedure, on which general business procedure is based, although there are variations, and what is correct in the House may not be necessary or desirable outside it.

There is no statutory law governing such procedure, but some aspects are influenced by certain laws such as the Public Meeting Act. To a great extent, it has evolved out of common usage and is thus not the law of the Medes and Persians but merely a framework designed to expedite the business to be transacted and within which any organisation, large or small, can plan its own rules, which must be designed to meet its special needs and the wishes of its members. For example, there are various ways of electing the chairman, secretary and committee members; each is equally correct. Every organisation selects its own method and incorporates the chosen system into its Rules – or Standing Orders – which then become the correct procedure for that organisation.

In the following pages, the various applications of procedure for different types of meeting will be explained, so that those with limited experience can confirm that they are following the right lines, and the novice may approach his first meeting with a clear head, though his heart may have sunk very low!

One often hears the negative remark, "I was asked to take the Chair, but had to refuse as I know nothing about it", and some of us must also have suffered from the chairman who has not been courageous enough to admit his limitations beforehand.

1

THE OFFICERS

THE CHAIRMAN

Chairmanship is an art and, like other arts, is developed and improved by training and practice.

In this book we refer to the chairman as 'he' though of course women are probably often better chairmen. Lady readers, please accept our apologies in advance, no slight intended, but it does make the book more readable.

A male chairman should be addressed as "Mr. Chairman" and a female chairman is correctly addressed as "Madam Chairman". We deplore the modern practice, seen in some 'progressive' organisations of addressing the chairman (of either sex) as 'chair'. The chairman is entitled to the dignity of being addressed as "Mr. Chairman", or "Madam Chairman", as appropriate, and is not to be referred to as a piece of furniture.

The position of chairman is an interesting and responsible one, well within the capacity of anyone who is keen on furthering the cause of his organisation and willing to take the trouble to study the relevant procedure.

Certain people obviously possess the necessary qualifications for chairmanship, but it is desirable to look for the following personal attributes:

1. A calm and friendly disposition.
2. The ability to think clearly and objectively.
3. A sound knowledge of procedure.
4. A sense of humour and *absolute* control of temper.

The duties of a chairman are mainly administrative, whereas those of a secretary are executive.

When presiding at a meeting, the chairman is responsible for its conduct, and it is for him to see that the business is properly carried out and that order is kept. His authority is almost absolute, so it will be appreciated that he should know how to use that authority to the best advantage.

Let us consider the qualities mentioned, with a view to understanding how they affect the smooth and efficient running of the organisation concerned.

1. *Temperament.* Holding an important and responsible position with control over the meetings through which the business of the organisation is transacted, it will be realised that the personality of the chairman and his ability to create the correct atmosphere must have a considerable influence on the whole structure. If he is friendly and a good mixer, others will follow his example and the general atmosphere will be friendly; but if he is inclined to be brusque and unapproachable, there will inevitably be cliques and factions.

A calm and even temperament is a great asset in a chairman as this creates a feeling of stability, whereas if there is too much volatility, the reverse is the case. Such a person is also more likely to remain unperturbed by a noisy meeting or difficult committee, and it is often only the efficiency of the chairman which prevents the complete breakdown of a meeting or the disruption of negotiations.

2. *Guidance.* The ability to think clearly and objectively is important, especially in committee work.

The chairman is, or should be, in a position to know all the ramifications of the business on the agenda and it is his duty to put all sides of the question to the members before a decision is reached. By withholding information, emphasizing one point or understating another in the initial stage of a discussion, or by a biased summing-up, he can often influence the result – a power which is open to abuse unless controlled by a clear brain and an open mind.

It is easy to influence people if one has knowledge and strong feelings about the matter under discussion. The wise chairman will endeavour not to push his personal views until his opinion is sought, but present the facts and information at his disposal as clearly as possible, leaving the meeting to make its own decisions.

Our whole system of procedure is designed to produce

democratic government, whether it be in the House of Commons or on the local Music Festival Committee, and this purpose is largely destroyed if the chairman arrogates to himself the role of dictator. His function is to inform and advise but not to direct decisions, otherwise why have committees and conferences at all?

3. *Meeting Control.* Obviously, if a chairman is to carry out his function effectively, he must know the correct procedure for the type of meeting over which he is to preside. General rules for each of the various meetings are given later in this book, and the beginner should study them carefully. It should be emphasized that, in addition to general procedure, he should possess a sound knowledge of the rules – or Standing Orders – laid down in the constitution of his particular organisation, as these take precedence over any other forms of procedure.

Frequently, one hears correct procedure condemned as being stereotyped, "red tape", detrimental to discussion, a waste of time and destructive of friendliness. These accusations are based on fallacies. A well-run meeting will get through more business, waste less time and give greater opportunity for free speech and sound decisions than the haphazard affair where everyone talks at once, or one or two people are allowed to hold the floor to the detriment of the tempers of all the rest. How many of us have probably abstained from voting because we were not sufficiently clear on the point at issue?

4. *Humour and Self-Control.* Perhaps one of the most difficult things with which the average chairman has to contend is his own temper; but self-control in this respect is vital to the successful management of any meeting. He should remember the value of humour as an antidote to rising tempers. To paraphrase a well-known saying: "A witty answer turneth away wrath", and the chairman who has this gift is indeed fortunate.

As has been said, audiences take their tone from the presiding officer, and irritability or loss of temper by the chairman will react adversely on the meeting. Tempers can easily become frayed from all sorts of outside causes, but nothing has a more stabilizing effect than a leader who refuses to get "rattled".

The authors saw a very good example of effective chairmanship at a big political meeting, where feeling was running high. Interrupters refused to allow the speaker to make himself heard, so instead of trying to shout them down, he quietly sat down, leaving the chairman to restore order. The chairman stood up, but made no attempt to quell the uproar; instead, he stood behind his table, calmly regarding the audience. After a few moments, the hecklers realized that they were getting nowhere, and the noise gradually subsided. The chairman waited until there was complete silence, then calmly asked: "Do you want Mr. — to continue his talk or not? It is all the same to us." This was so evidently true that the rest of the speech was heard in silence. Had either speaker or chairman shown any signs of agitation or temper, that meeting would have been doomed. Naturally, disrupted meetings do not always end so happily; that this one did was entirely due to the personality of the chairman.

Basic Rules of Chairmanship

The usual procedure followed at public committee and annual general meetings, conferences, debates and discussions, will be dealt with under the appropriate chapters; but a few universal rules governing all types of meetings may be helpful.

1. The chairman, by virtue of his office, takes precedence over all others present at the meeting over which he is presiding.

2. His ruling on any matter of procedure is final. Should the meeting lose confidence in the chairman, the method of ejecting him from office is as follows:

A member of the meeting must move a motion "That this meeting has no confidence in the chairman", which must be seconded and put to the meeting – usually by the secretary. If the resolution is carried by a large majority the chairman must vacate the chair. The meeting will then either close or elect another chairman to complete the business. Needless to say, this is a very unusual occurrence, but provides some measure of protection against inefficiency or unscrupulous behaviour.

The resolution of "No confidence" operates for one meeting

only, but would very probably be followed by the resignation of the chairman, otherwise a most uncomfortable state of affairs would ensue. Note that the majority required is a large one.

3. The chairman usually has a casting vote, to be used only when the voting for and against the motion is equal. If he is wise he will use his vote to support the *status quo*. A resolution carried against such strong opposition seldom operates well, whereas if it is rejected it leaves the situation open and the whole matter can then be re-considered at a subsequent meeting.

4. If offering himself for re-election, the chairman should not preside during the actual period when the election is taking place. He should absent himself to allow unhampered discussion, and the vice-chairman or a temporary chairman takes his place. If he is re-elected, he would normally return to the chair to preside over the rest of the meeting in the usual way.

5. The chairman should always stand to address the meeting, except in committees, and even then it is often desirable.

6. The chairman should insist that all questions, comments and observations made by any member of an audience or committee *must* be addressed to the chairman and not directly to the speaker or to anyone else in the room. Except at a committee meeting, the speaker should stand. This rule applies to all meetings, and the chairman who fails to enforce it will quickly lose control of the audience. While being addressed, the chairman should sit down, as the rules of chairmanship do not permit anyone else to speak while he is standing. This gives him some control over the speakers, as the mere fact of his rising to his feet should enforce immediate silence.

The correct phraseology for addressing the chair is: "Mr. Chairman, will the speaker tell us ..."; "May I ask through the chair ..."; or, at a committee meeting, "Mr. Chairman, may I ask ...". The actual wording matters little, provided the question is definitely put through the chairman.

Unless the questioner stands, it is almost impossible, in a large meeting, to see who is speaking. The chairman should be sure that no one wishing to speak is overlooked, as this creates a feeling of frustration and may give offence.

7. The appropriate procedure should be used at all times, however small and friendly the meeting. If members do not know it, they will quickly learn and appreciate the resulting efficiency and saving of time. Members attending business meetings should be expected to know the rules of the organisation.

8. Meetings should begin punctually and close formally, so that everyone is quite clear when the business is concluded. The chairman says "I declare the meeting closed at ..... p.m."

9. The chairman should work in close contact with the secretary. The two offices are complementary, not interchangeable, and the chairman is neither a dictator nor a passenger.

A Few Do's and Don'ts

Be brief – a long-winded chairman is a menace. Learn to focus the point of what has to be said and express it clearly and concisely.

Learn to suffer fools gladly, and avoid impatience or sarcasm, especially with shy and nervous people, as they may be too intimidated to speak again.

Cultivate a pleasant expression and be careful not to go into a coma when listening to a dull speech. Remember, the chairman is in full view of the audience and they will react to his attitude.

Audiences resent a careless appearance, so pay particular attention to personal details.

Avoid fidgeting, as idiosyncrasies and mannerisms divert the concentration of the audience.

Do not lean on the table – this looks weak-kneed and does not inspire confidence. It is also bad for the voice, which follows the eyes, and the chairman who does not stand properly is often inaudible. Cultivate an upright position, push the chair back, and stand clear of the table.

When using a microphone, speak clearly and quite softly, as you would when holding an ordinary conversation. Adjust the instrument to the level of your mouth, and stand 45-60cm (18 in to 2 ft) away.

Above all, know what should be done and see that it is done properly.

THE SECRETARY

The secretary of any organisation has a most interesting and important position. The smooth and efficient working of the society depends upon him; he (or she) is the hub from which the various activities radiate, and he has more to do with the practical running of the society than any other officer. Incompetence in this office can therefore seriously impede the work of the organisation.

As in the case of a chairman, when appointing a secretary, certain characteristics should be borne in mind. A secretary should be:

A good organiser.
Tidy and methodical.
Calm and clear-headed.
Tactful and friendly.

The duties of the secretary are purely executive, and he should keep in close contact with the chairman. It is his job to organise the routine office work, deal with all correspondence, convene all meetings, draw up agendas with the chairman, take minutes, write the annual report, carry out the instructions of his committee and give information and help to any member when required.

It will be appreciated that the duties of a secretary are varied as well as interesting, so, as the very variety may be a little frightening to the novice, let us consider them in greater detail.

Office Organisation

In a large society, there will be properly equipped offices, with one or more typists and possibly other helpers. The routine will be based on that of a business concern, in which case the secretary will probably be a fully-trained, paid official. Alternatively, a large number of organisations do not need such a structure and the secretary is a voluntary part-time worker, doing the business either from his own home or from a small office elsewhere. It is to this voluntary worker that a few hints may be useful.

Have a definite place in which to keep the books and papers of the society, and do not allow them to get mixed up with anything else. To simplify this, there should be a few items of office equipment such as:

A folder for letters awaiting attention.
A folder for the business concerning each committee.
A lettered concertina file for correspondence.
A postage book.
A minute book for each committee or sub-committee.
An account book for petty cash and a cash box in which to keep the money.
A typewriter, or word processor, or else a computer with a word processing package.
An alphabetical card index for members' names and addresses if these cannot be kept on computer.

Whatever system is adopted, it should be simple, methodical and tidy so that, should the secretary meet with some sudden accident, or be obliged to give up his work without adequate warning, someone else can take over and the work be carried on without undue disruption.

If the secretary has an office elsewhere than in his own home, he should endeavour to set aside a definite time during each week when he will be available to any members who may wish to contact him.

Correspondence

Whenever possible, letters should be answered within twenty-four hours, but in no case should they be allowed to remain unanswered for more than a week. Money should always be acknowledged by return of post.

A copy of the replies to all letters should be made and attached to the original before filing. If, however, a copy is not practicable, a note of the reply and the date should be made on the letter.

Unless the secretary's name appears on the heading of the notepaper, a woman should always give her prefix (Mrs., Miss) when signing letters, e.g. A.C. Smith (Miss), Alice Smith (Mrs., or Ms.); initials with no prefix presuppose that the writer is a man.

A postage book should be kept, in which all letters, both received and despatched, are entered on the correct date. This saves many an argument in tracing the last letter and, if accurately carried out, can also keep the postage account straight.

Petty Cash

The secretary will need petty cash for current expenses such as postage, etc. This should be obtained from the treasurer, and a careful account must be kept of all expenditure. It is also advisable to have a cash box with a lock. It is an axiom of law and good management never to mix personal monies with those held in trust for others.

Bills for amounts of more than twenty pounds or so are usually paid by the treasurer by cheque.

When the organisation is very small, or has few funds, the secretary may also act as treasurer.

Convening Meetings

It is the secretary's duty to send out notices – generally by post – of all meetings. Calling a meeting by telephone or personal contact is not correct procedure and mistakes as to time and date, etc., can easily arise. Plenty of time must be allowed. Dates will, of course, be arranged with the chairman. The agendas for committee meetings will also be drawn up by the secretary and chairman.

Minutes

Minutes are an accurate but condensed record of what takes place at a meeting, and it is the duty of the secretary to make this record.

Minutes must be taken at every meeting at which any business concerning the organisation is transacted. They are always necessary for a committee meeting or annual general meeting, usually for a conference, but not for a public meeting, or debates and discussions, though some regular debating societies and discussion groups do record their meetings in this way.

Inexperienced secretaries are often rather worried about the method of taking minutes and what to put in them.

There are various ways of taking minutes. A big organisation might tape-record the whole meeting or even have a shorthand writer to take it down *verbatim.* This will then be typed out and from it the secretary will make a précis for the minutes. The more usual method is for the secretary to make notes during the meeting and write up the record afterwards; but if this is done, the minutes should be written up as soon as possible, whilst the proceedings are still fresh in mind.

Minutes must be condensed and to the point. Perhaps it will clarify what should be put into them if they are regarded as a history of the society. They must therefore record all important facts and the outcome of discussions, but details of the actual discussion and irrelevant chat should be omitted. For instance, it is not necessary to record what Mr. — said, and that Mrs. — disagreed with him, only the ultimate decision arrived at by the meeting.

The wording of resolutions and amendments must be recorded in full and the name of the proposer and seconder given, whether they are eventually carried or not.

The construction of minutes follows a fairly usual form and will be on the following lines:

1. *Description of Meeting* (i.e. whether committee, sub-committee, annual general meeting, ordinary general meeting, conference, etc.) and the place, time and date on which it was held, e.g. "A meeting of the executive committee of the — Tennis Club, was held at 6 p.m. in the club-room on 8th August (year)."

2. *Those Present.* The name of the chairman should always be given. Other names, if a small meeting; otherwise the number, e.g. "Chairman: Mr. S—.

"Those present:..." or "49 members present".

3. *Apologies for Absence.* In a small meeting, all names should be recorded; in a large one, the names of any officers or leading members and the number of the remainder, e.g. "Apologies for absence were received from..."

4. *Minutes of the Last Meeting.* These will either be read or have been photocopied and circulated to members, e.g. "The minutes of the last meeting were approved by the meeting and

signed by (the chairman)."

5. *Business arising out of the Minutes.* This is merely a report of action taken as the result of decisions made at the last meeting. (In no case, of course, should any discussion have taken place.) E.g. "Mrs. S— reported that her husband is willing to lend his field for the fête on 6th September. Mr. W— reported that Sir John — regrets he is unable to open the fête. The secretary reported that S. & S., caterers, can supply teas at £3 per head for the fête."

6. *Reports* (if any) from sub-committees, treasurer, etc., e.g. "The Chairman of the Tournament Sub-Committee reported that..."

7. *Further Items.* Then follows a record of the result of discussion on other items of business before the meeting, e.g. "A resolution was proposed by Mr. — and seconded by Mr. —, 'That a new groundsman be appointed.' An amendment was proposed by Miss —, seconded by Mr. — and carried, 'That the words, At a weekly wage of £250, be added.' The amended resolution: 'That a new groundsman be appointed at a weekly wage of £250' was carried by a large majority." E.g. "The question of a new motor mower was discussed but no decision was reached."

After being drafted, the minutes should be shown to the chairman for approval and are then dealt with by being photocopied (to enable a copy to be sent to each member) and put into the minute book.

The minutes should be available to any member, but no one else can claim to see them as a right.

Reports

The writing of reports requires a clear and logical mind coupled with knowledge of the matter to be reported, but is not difficult.

A report is a statement of fact, a history of work dealt with by the organisation, and should be brief and interesting.

Every organisation, however small, should have its annual report, which is the account of the year's work presented by the committee to the members at the annual general meeting. It is the duty of the secretary to compile this report, in which he is usually assisted by the chairman.

When reading reports, attention should be paid to delivery; how often have we all listened – or tried to listen – to the mumbled, garbled reading of documents, the contents of which we have failed to grasp because we were unable to hear properly?

Reports and minutes should always be read standing, with the script held well up so that the head is not bent, as this causes the voice to travel downwards, with the result that only those in the immediate vicinity can hear.

Stand quietly and avoid fidgeting with the feet or hands. Read clearly and slowly and do not be afraid to pause at the end of a sentence or paragraph. The wise secretary makes himself thoroughly familiar with whatever he has to read, so that he can give words and phrases their proper value, and does not need to keep his eyes glued to the script, but can look up at the audience from time to time while finishing a sentence.

Carrying Out Instructions

The secretary must always carry out the instructions of his committee, whether he personally agrees with them or not.

It is within his province to decide details of office administration, but he must not make any decision affecting the work of the society without consulting the chairman and/or committee, unless empowered to do so. When a secretary has proved himself competent, he is often given considerable freedom in this respect, but it is not his by right of office.

Giving Information

In many cases the secretary finds himself in the position of liaison officer between the ordinary members and the committee and other officers – an interesting aspect of his work but one requiring tact and discretion! He is often the receptacle of grievances and complaints, as members will frequently tell him these in the hope that he will report them in the proper quarter; tact and understanding are needed to know when this should or should not be done. On many occasions, the secretary is able to smooth over difficulties and prevent misunderstandings, but he must exercise great discretion to ensure that he is neither guilty of any breach of confidence nor gives away inside information.

It will be appreciated how greatly the secretary can influence the running and atmosphere of the organisation and, conversely, how much harm can be done by slackness and indiscretion.

Procedure

As with the chairman, it is essential that the secretary should have a sound knowledge of common procedure and of the rules of his organisation.

Details of the procedure used in different types of meetings will be found within the appropriate chapters, but a few general rules affecting the secretary may be helpful.

1. The secretary should not give his personal views at a meeting unless asked to do so by the chairman.

2. Whether or not the secretary has a vote will be laid down in the rules of the organisation. Roughly speaking, this depends upon the method of his election. If he is elected at the annual general meeting to the office of secretary, he will not have a vote; but if he is first elected as a member of the committee and subsequently made secretary by that committee, then he will have a vote (see Chapter 8).

3. The secretary does not take the chair in the absence of the chairman except to get a substitute appointed, as in the case of a vote of "No confidence" in the chairman, or some sudden emergency.

4. If in doubt on any point, the secretary can, and should, ask the chairman to clarify what has been decided before passing on to the next item, as he must be quite clear on the matter if the minutes are to be accurate.

5. In some voluntary organisations it is considered courteous for the secretary to offer his resignation to the members if the chairman is retiring. This will probably not be accepted but gives the new chairman an opportunity to nominate someone else if he wishes. There is no rule on this point and it must be left to the discretion of the secretary to make the gesture, or not, according to circumstances.

THE TREASURER

The treasurer is responsible for the financial transactions of the society. In a large organisation, this entails considerable work, but in a small one, the post is not onerous.

His duties are to collect subscriptions, pay bills, scrutinize expenditure, keep the books, inform the committee of the financial position, prepare the statement of accounts for the annual general meeting, advise on the raising of funds for special purposes and on finance generally. He is responsible to the members for the proper transaction of all financial business, but not for the actual raising of money; this will be done by the executive committee, or by a finance sub-committee, appointed by them, of which the treasurer may possibly be the chairman.

Book-Keeping

In a big organisation, the treasurer will be experienced and probably trained in accountancy, but for the small society, a complicated system of book-keeping is unnecessary, and a tidy mind with the ability to deal accurately with figures are adequate qualifications. No great array of books is required. A Receipt Book, with carbons or counterfoils, a good-sized Cash Book (A4 is suitable), a Postage Book, a lettered file for correspondence and one for vouchers (receipts for outward payments) will be the only essentials at first.

It is advisable, even for a small fund, to open a bank account. This should be in the name of the society and preferably at a different bank from that used by the treasurer personally, to avoid the possibility of confusion.

Subscriptions should be sent to the treasurer and a receipt – written in ink or ball-point – given for every item, however small. A list of names and addresses of subscribers will be needed, and this can be obtained from the secretary, but it is better for the treasurer to have his own. Care must be taken to differentiate between a subscription and a donation, or subsequent confusion may arise.

A subscription is the payment of a defined amount at stated intervals in exchange for some benefit – as, for example, the membership of a society. A donation is a separate gift without reciprocal benefit and is not regular.

There is no definite rule as to the layout of the Cash (or Day) Book. The headings Receipts and Payments, or Debit and Credit are equally correct; receipts should be entered on the left and payments on the right.

Enter *details* of items in the book and on the receipt and cheque counterfoils, especially of payments for which there are no vouchers, e.g. "Miss S. —: salary £240, less... insurance... income tax... pension, etc."

Number all receipts for money received and vouchers for bills paid, and enter the numbers in the Cash Book; this makes subsequent checking much easier. Vouchers must be obtained for all items over £5.

Receipts for cheques are not necessary unless requested specifically by the sender, who may need one for his own records.

File all vouchers, to which the relevant detailed accounts have been attached; do not file "Accounts Rendered".

Avoid all "contra accounts", that is, one item offset by another. All money received and every item of expenditure must be shown, e.g. Mrs. Smith owes two pounds for her subscription but has spent £1 from her two pounds on behalf of the society. Do not subtract £1 from her two pounds and enter up: "Mrs. Smith: subscription £1"; the two pounds must appear under Receipts and the other items under Payments.

The Cash Book should be kept up to date and reconciled with the Bank statements at frequent intervals so that the financial position can be readily given.

Sample Page for Cash Book

RECEIPTS

Date *Aug.*	Rct. No.	Entry	£ p
1st		*Brought forward*	50.21
5th	47	Mrs. Smith: Annual Subscription	20.00
7th	48	Mrs. Sellers: Donation	5.00
8th	49	Mr. Soames: Balance on annual show	37.22
8th	50	Sale of literature at show	12.46

PAYMENTS

Date *Aug.*	Rct. No.	Entry	£ p
1st		*Brought forward*	27.21
7th	30	Secretary for Petty Cash	25.00
7th	31	Mrs. Smith: Crockery replacements	2.60
9th	32	W.H. Smith: printing headed paper	28.24
12th	33	Roote & Co.: repairs to Clubroom roof	728.00

In larger organisations some of the treasurer's functions may be carried out on a computer. There are many suitable accounting packages which will run even on relatively low-priced home computers.

Financial Statements

The treasurer must keep the committee regularly informed of the financial position. It may not be necessary for him to attend every meeting personally, but he should send a short statement to the secretary. The balance in hand and the approximate amount of liabilities will probably be all that is required.

He has the right to query expenditure but cannot control it; that is the committee's responsibility. He will be well advised to ensure that any large or unusual expenditure is properly authorised and recorded in the minutes. Should he feel the committee is adopting a financial policy against the interests of the society, and disregarding his protests, he can ask the chairman or president to call a general meeting and lay the matter before the members.

Every three or six months a balance sheet should be drawn up. If this is done regularly, it facilitates the preparation of the annual statement of accounts for the annual general meeting.

When preparing a statement of receipts and payments, first check all receipts against the Receipt Book counterfoils and all payments against the bank statement, or vouchers in the case of payments made from petty cash. Check the vouchers to ensure that all are to hand and correctly numbered, etc. If book-keeping is accurate, the preparation of a simple statement will not prove difficult, and a sample is given opposite. The balance in hand is obtained by deducting payments from receipts; and the resulting amount should tally with the money in the bank plus any cash in hand.

Sample Quarterly Statement of Receipts and Payments 1st April to 30th June (year)

RECEIPTS			PAYMENTS		
		£ p			£ p
Balance at bank, 1st April		500.00	Secretary, Petty Cash		50.00
Subscriptions:			*Printing:*		
Mrs. Williams	£30.00		Annual Report	£160.00	
Mr. Thomas	30.00		Notepaper	82.40	
Miss Smith	15.00				242.40
Mrs. Hardy	17.00		Donation to show fund		50.00
		92.00	Balance at bank, 30th June		356.60
Proceeds from sale of Annual Report		57.00			
Mrs. Black, donation to show		50.00			
		£699.00			£699.00

Any organisation which draws money from the public must, by law, submit a statement of accounts to its members once a year, at the annual general meeting. These accounts must be audited and the account books open to inspection at the meeting. A large concern will employ chartered accountants for the audit, but this is unnecessary for small organisations; any responsible person with a knowledge of accountancy is adequate, though it is advisable that he should not be closely connected with the treasurer. The auditor will require access to all the books, including the secretary's Petty Cash and Postage Books. These accounts should be brought up to date and closed in readiness.

There is no universal rule as to when the financial year shall end; each society decides this to suit its own conditions.

The annual statement of accounts – or Balance Sheet – is similar in construction to the quarterly statement but is less detailed.

After being passed by the auditors and approved by the annual general meeting, the statement will appear at the end of the annual report, together perhaps with the list of subscribers.

Sample Statement of Accounts for Year Ending 31st December (year)

RECEIPTS	£ p	PAYMENTS	£ p
To Balance in bank, 31st December (previous year)	2203.20	By Rent of office	3000.00
" Cash in hand, 31st December (previous year)	22.40	" Printing	506.00
" Subscriptions	4480.00	" Postage	245.00
" Donation	100.00	" Stationery	143.00
" Branch Contributions	500.00	" Entertaining	104.00
" Sale of literature	640.00	" Lectures, fees and expenses	463.00
" Advertisements in Annual Report	90.00	" Secretary's expenses	200.00
		" Literature	500.00
		" Donation to show	100.00
		" General expenses	142.00
		" Bank charges	20.00
		" Balance at bank, 31st December (year)	2460.29
		" Cash in hand, 31st December (year)	39.71
		" Stamps in hand, 31st December (year)	112.60
	£8035.60		£8035.60

Audited and found correct.

FRANK BURROUGHS.

12th January (following year)

2

PUBLIC MEETINGS

ORGANISATION

The Public Order Act of 1936 defines a public meeting as "any meeting in a public place and any meeting which the public or any section thereof are permitted to attend, whether on payment or otherwise" – in fact, every kind of meeting which is not restricted to members of the organisation only.

The purpose of such a meeting is to inform and instruct the general public on a particular subject. The object may be to raise money, increase membership, arouse interest, make some spiritual or material appeal, or to educate, but whatever the aim, it should be clearly borne in mind by the organisers. It is also as well to remember that people are seldom keen to attend such meetings and will be easily discouraged, so care must be taken to make attendance attractive and simple.

Many meetings fail through lack of preliminary organisation. Insufficient time is allowed for advertising and initial preparation, consequently the affair is muddled and lacks the smoothness which is attained by forethought.

The organisation of a public meeting is the responsibility of the committee concerned, but it is usual to allocate the detailed planning to a small sub-committee; the committee will provisionally decide the date, time and place of the meeting, suggest speakers and a chairman, and will then give the elected sub-committee power to proceed with further arrangements. Preparations should be made several weeks in advance.

Choice of Hall

In a village or small town, there is probably only one suitable hall, but where there is a choice, take the most central and the best known. In most towns, there is one particular building which has a certain standing and affords definite advantages. It may be more expensive but is worth the extra cost as people will not take the trouble to go to an out-of-the-way room. It is a good plan to include information about buses, and so forth, on the handbills.

It is better to have a small room full than a large one half empty, so endeavour to assess the possible numbers and do not be over-optimistic!

Speaker and Chairman

If a busy and eminent speaker is invited, it will be wise to give him a choice of dates. First ascertain if the hall is available and book it provisionally. A second choice of speaker should be made, to be contacted if by chance the original one finds he cannot come. When inviting a speaker always state the length of time he is required to speak and enquire as to the amount of his fee, or state what the society is prepared to offer; this will frequently save subsequent misunderstanding and embarrassment. When he accepts, ask for his biographical details for the chairman's benefit, and also if he cares to bring a précis for the Press.

The chair may be taken by the chairman of the organisation, but if not, select a chairman who fully understands what will be required of him. It is more important that he should be competent than well known, as a weak or inefficient chairman can ruin the success of the meeting.

Propose a timetable for the meeting and ask the chairman to keep to it. Allow five minutes for the chairman's opening remarks, thirty to sixty minutes (about forty is generally long enough) for the speaker, fifteen to thirty minutes for questions, and ten minutes for votes of thanks. This timetable is an indication only and will be adapted as required, but do not overload the programme or allow the meeting to drag on. The average person cannot concentrate fully for any prolonged period.

Advertising

Conditions are so varied that it is not possible to offer much advice on this subject. Expense is usually the deciding factor, but some outlay is essential for success. The usual method is to advertise in the local Press and to have as many posters and handbills as funds will permit.

The size of the poster will depend on the space available for display. Broadly speaking, large ones, properly billposted, are better for the town and small ones for fencing and gateposts in the country. In both cases, large lettering and the minimum of words will catch the eye.

Have plenty of handbills and put as much information as possible on them. Remember that the public has to be *encouraged* to attend a meeting, so make it sound as attractive as you can. Distribute the bills by hand. If they are sent by post, pushed under doors or through letter-boxes, they seldom receive attention, but if they are handed in personally, it ensures their being noticed. Such distributing takes time and organisation, but members and friends of the committee will usually help and it is well worth the trouble. The personal contact rouses interest and people are more likely to attend a meeting to which they, individually, have been invited. The best way of advertising anything is to talk about it. Always read handbills and posters very carefully before releasing them for distribution. Through failing to take this precaution, the authors once let the whole consignment go out with the speaker billed as "Mr. J. —, B.F." – an unfortunate printing error for a Bachelor of Arts!

A tour of the district with a car in which a loudspeaker has been installed is an additional way of publicising a meeting. Cruise very slowly, or stop at intervals. Do not shout into the microphone – though it is a great temptation to do so – but speak clearly, quietly and slowly. Be concise.

Press

A preliminary notice in the Press, followed later by paid advertisements, is one of the best forms of publicity. It is a good plan to get in touch with the editor of the local paper, either by letter or personal contact; tell him of the projected meeting and ask if he will give it a write-up or will accept one if it is sent in to him. Also request him to send a reporter to the meeting.

Detail a member to receive the reporter, show him where to sit and give him any information required. Obviously a reporter who is made welcome is more likely to take trouble than one of whom no notice is taken. He should be given, preferably in writing, particulars of the speaker, the names of the chairman, proposer and seconder of votes of thanks, and anyone else taking part. This ensures their inclusion and correct spelling in the report, should he leave before the end of the meeting.

Votes of Thanks

Those who are asked to propose and second a vote of thanks should be invited beforehand. It is extremely disconcerting to be called upon without warning. At a big meeting, they will have seats on the platform, but at a small one this is unnecessary and the proposal can be made from the floor. Under these circumstances, ask them to sit in front or at the end of a row so that they can step into the gangway and turn at an angle which will enable them to be heard from both platform and hall. Nothing is more irritating to an audience than being unable to hear. (See also page 37).

Particulars of Speaker

The secretary should obtain particulars of the speaker for the chairman. The information will be supplied by the speaker himself or his secretary; and a copy should be given to the chairman some days before the meeting to enable him to introduce the speaker correctly, and to the reporter at the meeting.

Stewards

For a large meeting, stewards will be necessary. They should be sensible, steady people, able to keep their heads in an emergency. Their duties will be to act as doorkeepers, count votes in a show of hands, remove anyone taken ill, take the collection (if any), see that the chairman's orders are carried out, and keep a general watch over the meeting. Divide the seating into blocks and allocate two or three stewards to each block. It is a good plan for them to wear some easily distinguishable mark, such as an arm-band; buttons and rosettes are often used, but cannot be seen from behind.

Arrangement of Hall

This is too often left to the caretaker, whose idea is usually to put the chairs as close together as they will go. Remember that discomfort causes fidgeting so see that the chairs are adequately spaced, with plenty of leg-room between the rows. If a large crowd is expected, they may have to be closely packed, but for every one occasion where this is necessary, there are twenty where it is not, and audiences suffer quite needless discomfort which also detracts from their powers of concentration.

Examine all means of ventilation and find which windows open and shut easily. All should, but they seldom do, and fussing with windows is distracting both to the speaker and audience.

Have the platform lighted from the front or side, as a light behind the speaker makes his face difficult to see. If the meeting is in a private room, see that he is not placed with his back to a window during day-time.

A lectern or a pile of books on the table at a suitable height for notes is a great help to many speakers, and there should be sufficient light to enable him to see them – a point frequently overlooked in the small meeting. Water and a gavel should also be supplied.

Test the microphone. The authors had a most upsetting experience owing to lack of this precaution. Every word "came back" immediately after being spoken, to the complete confusion of both speaker and audience; all efforts at adjustment failed and the equipment had to be disconnected. Subsequent investigation showed that the amplifiers had been fixed in the roof beams *facing* the platform, "because they fitted better that way"; so if the apparatus has been hired and installed by a kind friend who is not a professional – test it first.

It is usual to put the Press table either immediately below or to one side of the platform as the reporters must be able to see and hear clearly.

If preparations for refreshments are being made during the meeting, impress on the workers the need for quietness and closed doors.

Platform Precedence

At a large meeting, where there may be several people on the platform, the order of seating should be arranged beforehand. The chairman must sit in the centre, so that he can run the meeting properly. The person who sits in the middle can always dominate. There is nothing more pathetic to see than a chairman trying to control a rowdy meeting from an 'off-centre' position. As a general rule, the most important person will be placed to the right of the chairman, the next in importance on his left, and so on, right and left. It is not possible to give a table of precedence, as this depends on many factors; but the following suggestions may help.

A mayor attending officially in his own city or borough takes precedence over everyone except reigning Royalty. If the meeting be a county one, the Lord-Lieutenant of the county would be officially the most important person; if an ecclesiastical gathering, the Bishop of the Diocese would have the place of honour.

Some large towns which have a Lord Mayor, Lord-Lieutenant, Lord Bishop and, periodically, a High Court Judge or other highly-placed officials based there, have their own rules of precedence and advice can be obtained from the Chief Executive.

At an ordinary public meeting, the speaker is considered to be the guest of honour and, unless the mayor is present officially, will be on the right of the chairman. The probable arrangement will be: the speaker, with the proposer of the vote of thanks and the treasurer on the chairman's right; on his left, the supporting speaker, the vice-chairman and the seconder of the vote of thanks. The secretary can sit at either end or immediately behind the chairman, which is rather better, as he is then easily accessible.

At a small meeting, the chairman will have the speaker on his right and the secretary on his left, though the latter is not obliged to be on the platform if he is needed elsewhere.

The chairman will escort on to the platform those who are to sit on either side of him, and the secretary and organisers will deal with the remainder. It saves confusion, at a large meeting, to label the chairs.

PROCEDURE

Chairmanship

The chairman of a public meeting is responsible for its conduct. He is the liaison between platform and audience, and is responsible for keeping order. His duties are not difficult: the procedure is approximately the same whatever the size of the meeting, and provided that he is familiar with it, he has little to fear.

Let us consider a typical timetable for a small public meeting such as a beginner may have to tackle.

7.30 p.m. Meeting opened by chairman.
7.35 " Mr. W.— speaks.
8.15 " Questions to speaker.
8.45 " Vote of thanks proposed by Mr.—
Seconded by Mrs.—
Speaker's reply.
8.55 " Chairman closes meeting.

If the purpose of the meeting is to obtain the views of the audience on a specific matter, this will be incorporated into a carefully-worded motion, and there will be at least two speakers, one to propose and the other to second the motion. The resolution will then be put to the meeting after question time, and the vote taken by a show of hands.

Chairman's Opening Remarks

There are six points for a chairman to remember in his opening remarks, which should be prepared beforehand:

1. To welcome the audience.
2. To mention the work of the society (for public purposes).
3. To stimulate interest in the subject and to read the motion (if any).
4. To introduce the speaker.
5. To refer to question time.
6. To call on the speaker.

1. The purpose of welcoming the audience is to create a friendly atmosphere. Only a few words are necessary, but they should be sincerely and pleasantly spoken, and should not

sound like mere routine.

2. It is a good plan to refer to the organisation responsible for the meeting. Mention *very briefly* its object in holding it and touch lightly on any recent interesting activities. The reason for this is threefold. If there are reporters present, it provides them with material for a write-up and is good publicity. It conveys to any strangers present the fact that the society is a virile, active concern which will encourage recruits. It keeps members up to date and makes them feel they belong to a lively organisation which is achieving results.

3. The chairman is responsible for arousing interest in the speech. He must on no account encroach on the function of the speaker by talking on the subject – as is done all too frequently – but should merely link it up with local interests and conditions so that the audience feels it is about to hear something of immediate concern to itself.

4. Introducing the speaker is really "building him up" and for this purpose his "history" will have been obtained beforehand. By stating his qualifications of training, position and experience, his authority for speaking on that particular subject is guaranteed to the audience. This is a great help to the speaker and should not be omitted even if he is well known. The very frequent "You all know Mr —; he does not need any introduction from me" is poor chairmanship. Even if 99 per cent of the audience do know him, the remaining 1 per cent do not, and some of the ninety-nine may be very vague or inaccurately informed. So do not omit this introduction under any circumstances. Be accurate and do not eulogize. If there is more than one speaker, each will have to be dealt with similarly.

5. If possible, allow time for questions at the end of the speech. Explain this to the audience and ask them to refrain from interrupting the speaker. If they know that time has been allocated for questions, people will listen more contentedly and there will be less tendency to heckle.

6. The chairman then concludes by calling upon the speaker to address the meeting. These remarks should not take more than five minutes. Verbosity in a chairman is a deplorable vice. He must remember that the audience has come to hear the

speaker, and his duty is to interest them in the speaker and his subject and not to do or say anything to focus attention on himself. The following may be some guide to the kind of opening required:

"Ladies and Gentlemen. It is with very real pleasure that I welcome you all here this evening, as I feel sure we are going to have a most interesting and pleasant meeting.

"This society has always been particularly interested in encouraging the wider inclusion of the arts in education. At our last meeting, we heard of the progress made by our affiliated society in the United States of America, and I am sure you will all be interested to hear that we have been invited to send two members of this branch to attend their conference in Boston in November.

"The programme of arrangements and lectures for the next six months can be obtained from the secretary after the meeting.

"We are most fortunate in having as our speaker this evening, Sir James A—, who is going to talk to us on 'The Place of Music in Education'. Sir James is well known to most of us by name; he holds the highest degree in music and many of us will have listened with immense pleasure to his conducting of his own compositions. As an ex-schoolmaster of —, he is also well qualified to speak from the educationalists' as well as the musicians' point of view.

"The question of music in relation to education is surely one that affects nearly all of us closely. Those who are able to attend the cathedral services here will realise the heights of proficiency and appreciation which can be attained by quite young children. At the other extreme, the ceaseless bellowing of the radio to which we are so frequently subjected drives home the need for some sort of training in discrimination, if future generations are not to be tone-deaf.

"Sir James has very kindly said he will answer any questions you may care to put at the end of his talk, so will you save them up until then.

"I will now ask Sir James A— to speak to you on 'The Place of Music in Education'. Sir James A—."

Speech

At the average meeting, it is unlikely that there will be any interruptions and if there are, they will very often be due to forgetfulness. In this case, the chairman should just raise himself from his seat slightly and ask that the question is kept until the end. Whether the interruption is thoughtless or deliberate, do not allow the questioner to get away with it; deal with any such symptoms at once or they will develop. Should the disturbance continue, the chairman must rise to his feet, which will be the signal for the speaker to sit down, and he must cope with the situation until quiet is restored. He will then ask the speaker to continue. It is the chairman's duty to maintain order, not the speaker's, and if he is firm and remains calm, the occasions when he is likely to encounter trouble are few.

If the speaker looks like over-running his time, the chairman should give warning by putting in front of him a paper with "THREE MINUTES TO GO" in large letters written upon it. This is less noticeable to the audience than whispering and will give him time to conclude. Naturally the chairman will use discretion in this, but do not extend the time unless the audience is obviously enthralled.

Questions

When the speaker has finished, the chairman will call for questions. The manner in which he does this will make quite a difference as to whether they are forthcoming or not, so he must put his remarks in such a way that would-be questioners are encouraged. "After that most comprehensive speech, are there any questions?" is not likely to produce them; but something like "After that most stimulating talk, there are sure to be questions many of you will wish to ask" may produce results.

It must be clearly stated that the questioners must stand, be as brief as possible, and address the chairman. This is necessary to enable the chairman to see who wishes to speak and to make each questioner more audible. Brevity is essential if others are to have their opportunity, and extended remarks and observations should not be permitted. If there are likely to be many questions, a time limit for each should be fixed.

Addressing the chair is the golden rule that applies to all types of meeting and for which there are excellent reasons. It puts a curb on rising tempers. If a questioner puts his remarks directly to a speaker who may have aroused his animosity, the more he looks at him the angrier he will become, but if he has to address a benign, calm third person, his temper will tend to go off the boil. In this way, the chairman acts as a sort of insulator. The speaker should also reply through the chair. The questioner may be so placed as to be inaudible to those behind him, in which case the chairman should repeat the question for all to hear. If the question is badly phrased, the chairman should re-word it with the point clearly focused. Some chairmen make it a rule always to repeat the question, and this is possibly a good plan at big meetings, but not necessary at a small one.

The chairman should not accept unnecessarily offensive or abusive questions.

When several people rise to ask a question simultaneously, care must be exercised to ensure that each has his opportunity. The chairman will decide who speaks first, then take the others in turn. Indifference in this matter can cause a lot of bad feeling.

Verbal questions are preferable to written ones as they are more likely to hold the interest of the audience, but if a member is too nervous to speak, his written question can be handed to the chairman, who will read it aloud.

If questions are not forthcoming, as is frequently the case at small meetings, it is often encouraging if the chairman or one of the officers starts the ball rolling. An even better suggestion is to ask one or two members of the audience beforehand to be prepared to put some questions.

Votes of Thanks

When time is up or there are no more questions, the chairman will call upon whoever is giving the vote of thanks by name, "I will now ask Mr.— to thank our speaker." The speech of thanks will conclude with "I call on you all to join me in thanking our speaker" or some such phrase and start the clapping, the chairman synchronizing his applause.

This is now the more usual way of giving a vote of thanks rather than having a formal motion which needs to be proposed, seconded and put to the vote. If the formal method is preferred, the chairman will say "I will now call on Mr.— to propose and Mrs.— to second a vote of thanks to our speaker". After both have spoken the chairman will put the proposal to the meeting – "You have heard the vote of thanks proposed by — and seconded by –; will you now show your appreciation in the usual way" and lead the applause. (Seconding is often omitted but this is considered technically incorrect by some authorities and in any case deprives someone of the doubtful pleasure but indubitable practice gained from "saying a few words".)

The chairman may now quietly ask the speaker if he would care to reply to the vote of thanks, in which case it is considered courteous for him to do so, very briefly. It is also possible for the speaker to include thanks to the chairman at this point, which saves another vote of thanks and is a courtesy to be encouraged, especially at the smaller meeting. The secretary should mention it beforehand if the speaker is required to do this, and the latter will then conclude with some words as "I am sure you will all wish to join me in thanking the chairman for presiding so ably." At small meetings, when the chairman is usually an officer of the organisation, it is customary to pass a vote of thanks to the speaker only, unless the chairman has been specially invited to the chair when he should receive a vote of thanks separately, or jointly with the speaker, depending on circumstances.

Votes of thanks can become very wearisome if overdone, but are necessary for reasons of courtesy; when certain individuals have given time and trouble to help an organisation, the least it can do in return is to thank them publicly. At a smaller or more informal type of meeting, there may be no vote of thanks as such; instead the chairman simply thanks the speaker on behalf of those present. However, if a vote of thanks *is* proposed from the chair, it does not need seconding but can be put straight to the vote.

How to Propose a Vote of Thanks

For proposing a vote of thanks, a prepared speech is neither necessary nor desirable. The proposer should note any particular points made by the speaker and link them up with his remarks. His function is to stress points already made, not to introduce new ideas, and his appreciation should emphasize the facts of the speech rather than eulogize the speaker – which is embarrassing. The keynote is courtesy.

The highlight of a public meeting is the speech. It is the chairman's business to prepare the audience by focusing the spotlight on the speaker and his speech. The votes of thanks should re-focus the interest of the audience upon what has been said, and should never divert their minds by introducing new matter.

A light touch is good if it can be introduced without flippancy.

Should the proposer not agree with the speaker, he must not say so but use his tact to cover up this fact; it is always possible to express interest in a speech without necessarily agreeing with its sentiments.

Proposing a vote of thanks should not take more than three minutes, and it is better to make the formal proposition at the end, so that if the proposer "runs dry", he can conclude with the correct formal phrase.

To enable the nervous novice to begin fluently, write out an opening phrase and, if necessary, memorize it, e.g. "Mr. Chairman, Ladies and Gentlemen. I am really pleased to have this opportunity of expressing to our speaker (his name may be substituted) our appreciation of his most interesting talk. I feel sure you will all agree that... Mr. Chairman, I have much pleasure in proposing a sincere vote of thanks to the speaker."

How to Second a Vote of Thanks

Asking someone to propose or second a vote of thanks is a way of paying a small compliment, and is excellent practice for the potential speaker or chairman. The technique is the same as for the proposer, except that the time taken must be less; that is, not more than two minutes.

At a small meeting, it is not essential for the seconder to

make a speech but it is desirable that he should say just a few appreciative words, and it is excellent speaking practice.

End with the formal proposition: "It gives much pleasure to second the vote of thanks proposed by...". If nothing else is said, this phrase is adequate.

Closing the Meeting

After the vote of thanks the chairman will close the meeting. If he has any announcements to make or other matters to deal with such as thanking a hostess or helpers, he can do so at this point, ending with the formal closing, "That concludes the meeting." This is important and when omitted causes discomfort to the audience, which does not know whether to move about and talk freely or not, especially if the chairman and speaker do not immediately vacate the platform.

Although procedure is very straightforward, it is surprisingly easy to forget something, so the novice will be well advised to have notes. A card set out as follows will be a safeguard against mistakes and will give confidence. The lines between items are a reminder to sit down!

1. OPENING REMARKS
   Welcome.
   Publicity.
   Speaker.
   Rouse interest.
   Questions.
   Call on speaker.

---

2. ASK FOR QUESTIONS
   Standing.
   Through chair.
   Brief.

---

3. CALL ON PROPOSER OF VOTE OF THANKS

---

4. CALL ON SECONDER OF VOTE OF THANKS

---

5. PUT VOTE TO THE MEETING

6. ASK SPEAKER TO REPLY

7. CLOSE MEETING

Hecklers

Ordinarily, the chairman will have very little difficulty in keeping order. Most audiences have a strong sense of fair play and will side with him in suppressing interruptions.

At meetings of a highly controversial nature, however, such as politics, some heckling is to be expected, but so long as it remains good-humoured it can be dealt with. There is, however, a persistent type of interruption obviously intended to disrupt the meeting, which requires firm measures.

As soon as the chairman observes these intentions, he should appeal to the audience's sense of fair play and use his tact to secure order. If this proves unsuccessful, he must apply his powers of authority to deal with the interrupters.

Where meetings are held on private premises, that is, on premises to which the public have access only by permission of the owner, occupier or lessee, the audience, whether they have paid for admission or not, are there only by invitation of the conveners. This applies to all buildings and out-of-door meetings except those held on common land or in the street. Permission to be present can be withdrawn at any time by the chairman and anyone requested to leave the meeting must do so. If he refuses, he becomes a trespasser and reasonable force can be used to eject him; if he resists, the police can be called in.

If the meeting looks like degenerating into a brawl, the chairman can and should call in the police. He is empowered to do so by the Public Meeting Act of 1908 and the Public Order Act of 1936, which state: "Any person who at a lawful public meeting acts in a disorderly manner for the purpose of preventing the transacting of the business for which the meeting was called together shall be guilty of an offence" and "It is a general offence to use threatening, abusive or insulting behaviour at a public meeting whereby a breach of the peace might be caused."

If the police have to be called in by the chairman of the meeting, when they arrive they will proceed to ask the offenders for their names and addresses.

If the disorder makes it impossible to continue the meeting, the chairman can either adjourn it until order is restored or close it entirely; but to take the latter course is to play right into the hands of the interrupters, so it is better to adjourn until the upheaval has been dealt with and then to continue the meeting.

Forms of Address

When there are people of importance on the platform, it is usual for the chairman to refer to them by name in his opening remarks, e.g. "Mr. Mayor, My Lord, Ladies and Gentlemen." The speaker or anyone in the audience will always refer to the chairman first, e.g. "Mr. Chairman, Mr. Mayor, My Lord, Ladies and Gentlemen."

Unless the chairman is used to contacting a wide range of people, it is not always easy to think of the right mode of address. The authors were once at a meeting where the chairman was caught unprepared. On his right hand was the mayor and on his left a bishop. He started all right with "Your Worship", then turned to his left, looked helplessly at the bishop, stuttered, became very red and finally burst out "and our brother in God"!!

The following list may help to avoid such embarrassing moments:

Chairman	Mr. Chairman.
Woman chairman	Madam Chairman.
Mayor	Mr. Mayor or Your Worship.
Mayor's wife or acting hostess to Mayor	Mayoress.
Woman Mayor	Madam Mayor.
Daughter or acting hostess to Mayor	Mayoress.
Lord Mayor	My Lord Mayor.
His wife, etc.	Lady Mayoress.
Lady Mayor	My Lady Mayor.
President	Mr. President.
Woman President	Madam President.
Diocesan Bishop	My Lord or My Lord Bishop.
Suffragan Bishop	Mr. Bishop or Bishop.
Dean.	Mr. Dean.

Archdeacon	Mr. Archdeacon.
Canon	Canon—.
High Court Judge	My Lord.
Other judges	Judge or Mr. Justice.
Duke and Duchess	Your Grace.
All Peers and Peeresses below ducal rank	Lord—; Lady-.
Baronets and Knights	Sir J— S—.
Their wives	Lady S—.
The Honourable —	Mr., Mrs. or Miss.

Outdoor Public Meetings

Most outdoor meetings are held for propaganda purposes and range from those at street corners to large demonstrations.

Procedure at these is necessarily informal, the chairman's chief function being to attract the audience in the first place and subsequently keep it in good humour. A loudspeaker is a tremendous advantage, but do not speak from inside a closed car as the public like to see who is talking.

A few friends gathered round to form a nucleus helps to attract a crowd, but a special technique on the part of the chairman is called for. This does not require the usual opening procedure, but the use of cheap-jack methods and a glib tongue. Consider the types likely to be passing by – a mother, a housewife, a workman, a businessman, a boy and girl – and prepare some relevant patter likely to appeal to them, e.g. "That's a fine baby you have there, madam; do you realise how his future will be affected by...?"

People are curious and a small crowd will soon gather. When the chairman considers the audience sufficiently large, he will introduce the speaker very briefly and hand over to him. Speeches should be short and sustained argument avoided or people will drift away.

This type of meeting is an invaluable practice in dealing with a mixed collection of people, and calls for good humour and imperturbability, as heckling is inevitable.

3

FURTHER POINTS OF PROCEDURE

MOTIONS, RESOLUTIONS AND AMENDMENTS

There is probably nothing in the whole extent of meeting procedure which the beginner finds more terrifying than the prospect of dealing with motions, resolutions and amendments. Admittedly, the rules of debate can be rather complicated in their more advanced stages, but for ordinary purposes these technicalities are not necessary or desirable, and a sound working knowledge of this procedure is not difficult to acquire.

1. A Motion is a subject proposed as a basis for discussion.
2. A Resolution is the same motion after it has been voted upon, i.e. resolved.
3. An Amendment substitutes, adds or deletes words anywhere in the motion, but must not alter the basic intention of the motion.
4. An Addendum adds words to the end of a motion.
5. A Rider is also added at the end of a motion, usually in the form of a suggestion or recommendation.
6. A Counter Motion is an alternative motion for consideration.
7. A Counter Amendment is a drastic alteration in the application of the motion, while retaining its basic intention.

As the beginner is not likely to encounter the last two in the ordinary way, they will be explained at the end of this chapter.

Motions (or Proposals)

A motion is the term applied to an item of business or suggestion put forward for consideration at any meeting.

It must begin with the word "That", and express its meaning clearly and concisely.

The wording should always be in the positive; it must declare an opinion and preferably call for some action, e.g. "That smoking is detrimental to health and the Government be urged to curtail the practice."

A motion worded in the negative form is badly drafted, as no sensible person wishes to discuss a negative opinion, e.g. "That this meeting does not consider reorganisation of the police to be necessary and that a national basis would not be advisable." Such a motion can often be re-worded in a positive form, thus: "That this meeting considers that police forces should remain organised on a regional basis."

Before being amended, a motion is termed the *original* motion.

Resolutions

Motions and resolutions are not synonymous terms and there is much misunderstanding on this point. A motion does not become a resolution until it has been put to the vote and "resolved".

It is easy to see how this confusion has arisen. A meeting is called to consider a motion and passes it. It then becomes a resolution and, as such, is sent up to the higher authority. They, in turn, meet to discuss a motion which incorporates the resolution submitted to them for consideration. An inexperienced chairman probably says: "The *resolution* before the meeting is...", whereas he should say, "The *motion* before the meeting is 'That the following resolution be considered...' "; and so the mistake arises. Many people use the terms indiscriminately and organisations frequently send down resolutions instead of motions for consideration by branches

Amendments

These substitute, add or delete words anywhere in a motion, with the object of improving it. Their purpose is to incorporate in the motion the suggestions and opinions arising out of discussion.

They must be brief and not contrary to the meaning of the motion. A sample amendment might read as follows:

Original motion: *That this organisation holds a handicraft exhibition in the winter of 19—.*

Amendment No. 1: That the words *and festival of country dancing* be added after the word "exhibition".

Amendments can themselves be amended, but such amendments to amendments must apply only to the amendment and not to the motion itself. As an example, the words *in national costume* might be added to the previous amendment, making this: *and festival of country dancing in national costume.* This is called an "amendment to the amendment".

Amendment No. 2: A further alteration might be to delete the word *winter* and substitute *spring.*

and so on.

There is no limit to the number of amendments, but too many are confusing and it is often possible to incorporate two or three suggestions into one amendment with the consent of the proposers. This saves time and complication. Four or five amendments should be the absolute limit.

Addenda and Riders

These are really the same, as both only add words to a motion. For ordinary purposes, the word "amendment" covers every alteration, but some people prefer to be precise and will propose an "addendum" where they wish a word or words added.

A rider is an addition to the end of a motion, usually in the form of a recommendation. It can be put forward either before or after the motion is finally put to the vote. Example given on page 51.

Procedure

There are certain general rules governing the procedure for dealing with motions. These are subject to variation in different organisations, as each has its own ideas as to the precise way in which the business should be transacted. The procedures laid down in standing orders should be followed.

Standing order procedure usually requires that every motion or amendment be proposed (or moved) and seconded. At larger gatherings, seconding may be formal only ("I second formally, Mr. Chairman"), or possibly omitted altogether. However, if a seconder is required in the standing orders then any motion for which no seconder is forthcoming fails. No further discussion on it takes place and the meeting passes to the next item. Some rules of procedure require the motion to be seconded in writing in advance; some chairmen call for the seconder straight away. Others allow the mover of the motion to make his proposing speech, then call for a seconder. Seconding is desirable before discussion as it ensures that at least two people are in favour of the motion and prevents a member wasting time in discussing his personal hobby-horse.

Under some rules, however, a seconder is allowed to second formally immediately the proposer has spoken, with the right to make a more detailed speech at a later stage in the discussion.

Some organisations omit the seconding of motions in Committee. This usually saves time, but causes difficulty when somebody insists on discussing his pet idea.

Motions which are not controversial, such as votes of thanks, condolences, etc. should not need seconding. These are called "pious" motions, and can be put straight to the vote and carried *nem. con.* (without opposition), or by acclamation. If argument develops, however, a seconder must be obtained at once. Motions of a controversial nature should not normally be moved from the chair, as this detracts from the chair's impartiality. The proposer of an original motion has a right of reply – that is, the right to reply to the points raised during discussion immediately before the vote is taken. Some rules of procedure also give him a right to speak once, for or against, each amendment.

Subject to the standing orders, any member may normally propose or second an amendment. Sometimes he is allowed the same right of reply as the proposer of the original motion.

With the above exceptions members may usually speak only

once, for or against, each motion (or amendment). At small meetings, the rules may provide discretion to the chairman to allow members to speak a second time.

All speakers must address the chair. The usual formulae for proposing or seconding a motion or amendment are "Mr. Chairman I move (or propose) a motion that..." and "Mr. Chairman I have pleasure in seconding that motion (or amendment)".

During discussion, the chairman should call on members to speak for or against, alternately if possible, as this keeps the subject balanced. It also helps if the speakers announce which side they are taking by opening with a phrase such as: "Mr. Chairman, I rise to speak for (or against) the amendment."

Amending Motions

If a motion is thoroughly unpopular, no one will bother to amend it. It will be put to the vote, defeated and dropped; or the proposer and seconder may both prefer to withdraw it before the voting.

Motions must be amended clause by clause consecutively. It is a building-up process and to jump about would obviously confuse the members. If, for a good reason, it is necessary to revert to a previous clause, to amend it, the chairman must obtain the consent of the meeting. Where amendments are received in writing, as at a conference, this is not likely to happen, but can readily occur when amendments arise out of discussion. The chairman must keep a careful watch on this point.

Voting

Under no circumstances can voting on any matter take place unless a quorum is present, that is, a minimum number of members as laid down in the standing orders of the organisation.

There are two methods of voting upon amendments:

1. The original motion is proposed, seconded and discussed. The first amendment is proposed, seconded and discussed; amendments to the amendment are incorporated, if passed, and the final amendment is then put to the vote straight away.

If agreed, it is embodied in the original motion, which now becomes the substantive motion, showing that it has been altered.

Each amendment is dealt with in a similar manner, and finally the amended motion is put to the vote in its entirety.

This is the usual and most straightforward procedure when amendments have been received in writing; but at informal meetings, many suggested amendments may arise through discussion and the following method of sorting them out may be necessary.

2. The original motion is proposed, seconded and debated. Amendment No. 1 is moved, seconded and debated. Amendments to that amendment are proposed, seconded and discussed, then put to the vote at once; but the amendment in its final form is left to be voted upon later.

Amendment No. 2 is dealt with similarly, and so on until there are no further amendments. These are then put to the vote in turn, beginning at No. 1 and working outwards. Amendments that are passed are embodied in the original motion, which is then read in its amended form and put to the vote at the end.

Any motion for an amendment, or amendment to an amendment that is defeated is dropped and cannot be reintroduced at the same meeting.

There is some misapprehension about voting upon the finally amended motion (sometimes called the *main question*). People think that if they vote for an amendment, it presupposes acceptance of the original motion, which is not so. To refer to our example, a member may not want an "International handicraft exhibition" at all, but if he must have it, would rather have "a country dance festival" as well, so votes for that amendment even though he will vote against the whole plan eventually. For this reason, it is essential that the complete amended motion be put to the vote, when the dissenting member can vote against it.

The chairman should be sure that members know exactly what they are voting upon, and to be certain he should always read the motion or amendment before putting it to the vote. To say, "We will now take the vote on Amendment No. 1" is not sufficient. Some members may have recorded it in full, but he must consider those who have not done so. This also ensures that the wording is correct.

The most usual method of voting is by a show of hands. The chairman will ask those in favour to raise one hand. These will be counted and he will then ask for those against the motion. If the majority are in favour, the motion is passed and becomes a resolution; if the reverse, the motion is lost.

Other ways of voting are by voice, ballot or lobbying. The voice method is not accurate, as the chairman judges the result by the volume of sound emitted by the *ayes* and *noes:* which cannot be reliable in the case of close voting. Balloting is, of course, excellent but takes time; each member records his vote on a paper and hands it to the tellers, who are responsible for collecting and counting them. Lobbying, which is the parliamentary method, is also slow, members passing in single file out of two separate doors while the tellers count them, one door being for the *ayes* and another for the *noes.*

Should a member be dissatisfied with the conduct of the voting, he can demand a ballot. The chairman will decide whether this is justified or not and when it is to take place.

There is often inaccuracy in declaring the results of a vote. If every eligible person in the room votes in favour of a motion, then it is carried *unanimously.* If none vote against, but some abstain, it is carried *nem. con.* (Latin: *nemo contra,* no-one against). If only a few abstain or vote against, then it is carried by an *overwhelming majority.* With about a quarter of the votes against, it is a *large majority.* If voting is close, then it will be described as carried by a *majority* or a *small majority.* The number of votes for and against a motion should always be recorded in the minutes and in some cases a note should also be made of the number of abstainers, but this is not usually necessary.

Rescinding a Resolution

Once a motion or amendment has been voted upon, the resolution cannot be rescinded or altered unless a motion is moved for this purpose. This obviously cannot be done lightly or chaos would ensue, so most organisations lay down strict rules on the point, usually to the effect that it cannot be done at the same meeting and stating the time which must elapse before such a motion may be introduced.

There are occasions when subsequent events make a decision futile or harmful, necessitating its rescinding; but a resolution should be regarded as a decree not to be easily over-ruled.

Example of an Amended Motion

Original Motion

That this organisation holds an International handicraft exhibition in the winter of (year)

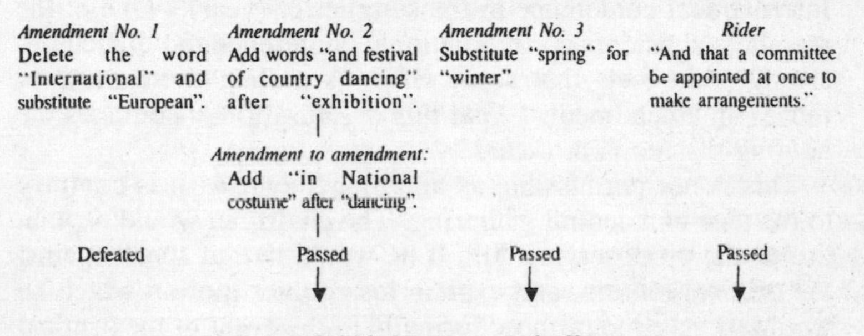

Amended Motion as put to the Vote

That this organisation holds an International handicraft exhibition *and festival of country dancing in National costume* in the *Spring* of (year) *and that a committee be appointed at once to make arrangements.*

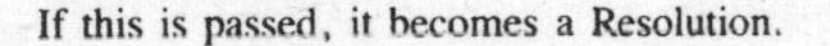

If this is passed, it becomes a Resolution.

Counter Motions and Counter Amendments

Having mastered the procedure for motions, amendments and the subsequent voting on motions which become resolutions, the beginner is well equipped for all ordinary meetings. There are, however, occasions when the feeling of the meeting is either against the original motion and desires to substitute a counter motion, or agrees with the basic idea but desires to alter the application drastically by means of a counter amendment, rather than improve it by slight amendments. It is well, therefore, for beginners to understand counter motions and counter amendments, though they seldom occur.

A Counter Motion. Except in the House of Commons, where the procedure is unique, an original motion cannot be thrown out by an amendment, and, as previously explained, no amendment may be contrary to the intention of the original motion. Incorrect amendments of this kind are frequently moved in ignorance and must not be accepted by the chairman, but if suitable, they should be put down – or tabled – as an alternative or "counter" motion, to be dealt with later if the one under discussion is defeated. As our example of this, the original motion might be "That this organisation holds an International conference in the summer of (year)." One of the members considers an International conference too difficult to arrange, but feels that some effort is perhaps necessary, so moves an amendment: "That this organisation encourages the holding of camps in (year)."

This is not permissible as an amendment, as it is contrary to the idea of a central gathering. The chairman would explain this to the proposer, ask him if he would like to speak against the original motion, and explain his counter motion which he would be asked to propose formally in the event of the original motion being defeated.

Example of Counter Motion

Original Motion:

That this organisation holds an
International conference in the summer of (year)

Amendment:

That this organisation encourages the holding of camps in (year)

Disallowed by chairman as contrary to original motion.
Tabled by proposer as counter motion.
No further amendments moved on original motion.
Original motion put to vote and defeated.
Counter motion put forward for discussion, now becomes

Original Motion:

That this organisation encourages the holding of camps in (year)

Open to further amendment in the usual way.

Counter Amendment. This is a time-saving method of drastically altering the application of a motion, while still retaining its original intention: an alternative suggestion on the same basic idea.

The counter amendment, duly proposed and seconded, is put to the meeting and, if passed, replaces the original motion as a basis for discussion. This is now termed the substantive motion, to show that it has been altered from the original, e.g. Original Motion: "That this organisation holds an International conference in the summer of (year)." Some member considers a conference dull and not what is required, though he heartily approves of an International gathering. He also feels that a winter meeting would be good for a change, so proposes: "That this organisation holds an International handicraft exhibition in the winter of (year)" – a counter amendment. It will be realised that this alters the whole application of the motion as obviously planning for a conference is entirely different from a handicraft exhibition; but the basic idea of an International gathering is retained.

The same result can, of course, be attained by amending in the ordinary way, but that is more cumbersome and takes longer.

Example of a Counter Amendment

Original Motion:

That this organisation holds an
International conference in the summer of (year)

Counter Amendment:

That this organisation holds an
International *handicraft exhibition* in the *winter* of (year)

Voted upon and passed, thus replacing the original motion and becoming the

Substantive Motion:

That this organisation holds an
International handicraft exhibition in the winter of (year)

Open to further amendment.

POINTS OF ORDER

A point of order must deal with the conduct or procedure of the meeting. A member cannot call a point of order because he disagrees with the speaker or chairman, though this is often done through ignorance of what constitutes a point of order, and sometimes with the deliberate intention of being tiresome both to speaker and chairman.

There are four bases upon which points of order can be called:

Incorrect procedure.
Irrelevancy.
Unparliamentary language.
Transgressing rules of the society.

Incorrect procedure implies that some member is contravening the rules of the conference or meeting, e.g.

speaking for longer than the time allowed, proposing an amendment incorrectly, speaking out of turn, and so on.

Irrelevancy is called when the speaker is wandering from the subject.

Unparliamentary language is not only bad language, such as swearing, personal abuse and so on, but innuendo implying something derogatory to a society, place or person and misrepresentation.

Transgressing the rules of the society means the use of procedure contrary to that laid down in the standing orders of the organisation. The making of any suggestion which is contrary to those rules or to some resolution passed at a previous meeting can be called on a point of order. Note that *incorrect procedure* is contravening the rules of that particular meeting, while *transgressing the rules of the society* applies to the procedure governing the conduct of the organisation and is therefore a much wider question, for which a sound knowledge of the standing orders is necessary.

Procedure

A point of order must be called immediately the mistake occurs and cannot be raised on a breach that has taken place some time before. It must be addressed to the chair and stated briefly. The usual phraseology is: "Mr. Chairman, on a point of order the speaker is..."; or "Mr. Chairman, is it in order to..?"; No speeches can be allowed and the chairman's ruling is final. If he considers the member is justified, he will correct the speaker accordingly; if not, he will disallow the protest. Should a large majority of the members disagree with the chairman, they can propose a vote of "No Confidence" and deal with the matter as stated in Chapter 1, but such a situation is unlikely to arise with a competent chairman.

If the interrupter is deliberately trying to disconcert the speaker and use up some of his time, he will probably attempt to argue the matter with the chairman. The speaker should resume his seat directly the point of order is raised and make a note of the time; then, if the argument is prolonged, he can ask the chairman to allow him the amount of time lost.

Sometimes unscrupulous opponents will distort or misquote

the remarks of the previous speaker, or there may be genuine misunderstanding as to what he said. In such cases, the misunderstood speaker can rise and say: "May I make a point of explanation, Mr. Chairman?" The chairman can allow this, but only a strictly relevant explanation can be permitted.

A point of order on procedure may be put to the chairman even when a member is not speaking, as the interjector may wish to ask some perfectly legitimate question about the routine of the meeting, the effect of the motion under discussion, or some other business.

The constant interruption of a meeting on points of order is to be deplored. They interfere with the business and, in most cases, are quite unnecessary as the chairman is – or should be – well able to deal with any serious departure from procedure.

CLOSURES

A closure is a motion moved for the purpose of stopping discussion. It cannot be proposed when someone is actually speaking or until the time limit for debate has expired. It must be seconded in the usual way and put to the vote at once without being discussed.

Although the chairman may use his discretion to close a debate, it is not always possible for him to exercise this right without laying himself open to the charge of being biased. There are, therefore, several ways in which members can put an end to discussion, each designed to meet a different requirement and result.

The most commonly encountered closures are:

Motion for the next business.
Motion that the question be now put.
Motion for referring back.
Motion for adjournment.

None of these closures can be moved by a member who has already spoken on the motion or amendment at issue.

1. *Proceed to next business.* This closure is used to end the discussion or to get the motion under review dismissed without a vote. Members may feel that there is not enough data

available to enable them to make a decision on the subject, or that it is not of sufficient importance to warrant a vote being taken. Someone will propose a motion: "Mr. Chairman, I beg to move a motion that we proceed to the next business". This is seconded and put to the vote, with either of the following results:

(a) If carried, no vote is taken, the subject is closed and may or may not be resumed later; and the meeting proceeds to the next item on the agenda.
(b) If defeated, discussion on the matter on hand is resumed; and the vote may or may not be taken.

2. *That the question be now put.* This closure is used to force a vote on the motion under discussion. It cannot be moved by the proposer or seconder of the motion – or amendment – under consideration. Members feel they have all the necessary information and that enough time has been spent in debate, so someone moves: "Mr. Chairman, I move that the question be now put."

(a) If carried, only the mover of the motion under discussion is allowed to speak again; then the vote is taken immediately.
(b) If defeated, discussion is resumed.

3. *Referring back.* This is commonly used in committee, or at any meeting which is discussing resolutions or reports submitted by satellite committees. Members do not like the matter as it stands, which may be ill-considered or not sufficiently detailed, so send it back for further attention to the body concerned, who will then either redraft the suggestion or let it drop, according to circumstances. "Mr. Chairman, I move that this matter be referred back to..."

(a) If carried, no further discussion takes place, and the motion is returned to its originators.
(b) If defeated, discussion is resumed.

4. *Adjournment.* A motion for adjournment may be moved for the purpose of (i) postponing discussion on a particular subject, or (ii) dispersing the meeting for a given period of

time. Debate on a motion might be adjourned pending the receipt of information; this might be to hand in half an hour or not for days. In the meantime, the subject is in abeyance, but not dismissed. On the other hand, a meeting may be adjourned for lunch, etc., but this is usually done by the chairman and should not require a motion. "Mr. Chairman, I move that this motion be adjourned until..."

When a motion for closure has been defeated, some time must elapse before it can again be proposed. The time limit is often stated in standing orders; if not, the chairman must use his discretion.

The standing orders, especially for large conferences, often provide the chairman with the right not to accept closure motions if he considers that there has been insufficient or unbalanced discussion.

Other closures are obscure and seldom encountered nowadays, but a devotee of archaic procedures might try to catch a chairman out with a *Motion for the Previous Question.* This is a very drastic closure, as its purpose is to avoid both decision and further discussion. It may not be moved on an amendment or in a committee meeting, and the chairman can refuse to accept it if he considers it inopportune, as whether it is carried or defeated, no further discussion is possible. It is applied by members who do not want the question at issue to come to the vote or to be discussed, and is often used to shelve an undesirable motion indefinitely. "Mr. Chairman, I move a motion for the previous question."

(a) If carried, no vote is taken and no further discussion takes place.

(b) If defeated, the vote is taken immediately, without further discussion.

4

CONFERENCES

FORMAL CONFERENCES

Organising and chairing a big conference requires considerable experience and it is unlikely that a beginner will be called upon to undertake such work. It is, however, probable that he will have to deal with an informal one, the procedure for which is a modified form of that given later in this chapter. For this reason, it is advisable for the novice to learn as much as possible of the organisation and procedure governing a formal convention. It is also likely that he may have to attend one as a delegate, when such knowledge will be very useful.

Whether a conference is large or small, its purpose is to "confer". It will be convened by an organisation to obtain the views of its members on certain definite subjects.

The difference between a public meeting and a conference is that the former is open to the public and usually promoted for propaganda purposes, whereas a conference is for members of a particular organisation only, and convened for discussion. At a public meeting, the public comes to listen and does not expect to do more than ask a brief question; but those attending a conference rely on having the opportunity of conferring, so that the policy under discussion can be strengthened by constructive criticism.

It is usual to have speakers on the various subjects, but their function is to explain the proposed policy and to answer questions upon it rather than to give personal opinions and experiences.

Initial Arrangements

When a large organisation wishes to hold a conference, its first move will be to describe the subjects upon which it wants the opinion of the members, and then to appoint a suitable sub-committee to deal with the arrangements. Members of this committee should have a thorough knowledge of the subjects to be discussed and should understand the drafting of motions, amendments and so on.

Begin making arrangements several weeks – or even months – before the date fixed for the conference. The subjects for discussion have to be circulated to the various branches either direct or through the area or county organisations, who must then discuss them and return their findings to the committee for incorporation in the agenda: and this takes considerable time.

There are two forms in which subjects for discussion can be presented to the branches: as suggestions for consideration and (if the broad outlines of policy have already been determined) as properly worded motions for amendment. The latter is the better method as it ensures clarity and is more likely to limit branch discussion to the matter in hand.

On receiving the motions, each branch will call its own conference or meeting, thrash out the questions, and return its opinions to the committee, if possible as correctly worded amendments. Naturally, where there are several branches, many of the amendments will be almost identical in meaning, if not in wording. The conference committee will then co-ordinate or consolidate these and send the final version to each of the branches concerned for approval. The amendments will then stand in the names of those branches.

Agenda

When all the amendments are to hand, the agenda will be drawn up. The subjects will need to be grouped and a separate session planned to deal with each subject or group of subjects. The agenda must be carefully timed and over-crowding avoided: many conferences are spoilt by too full a programme, which results in inadequate discussion and over-tired delegates. Probably half the value of a conference is derived from the free intercourse of delegates and this should be remembered in planning the programme.

The agenda for a two-day conference might be on these lines:

A Conference of the — Association will be held at ....
on Saturday and Sunday, 6th and 7th March (year).

AGENDA
Saturday, 6th March

10.30 *a.m.* *Opening session.*
Chairman: Sir William —, J.P., F.R.A.C.

11.00 *a.m.*–1.00 *p.m.* *Morning session.*
Motion before the conference: "That..."
Proposed by Mr. —.
Seconded by Miss —.
Chairman: Mr. W.S. Williams.
Special Speaker: Mrs. Sands, J.P.

2.30–4.00 *p.m.* *Afternoon session.*
To discuss the suggestion "That..."
Chairman: Mrs. Timon.
Speaker: Miss Holly (Chairman of Burns branch).

5.00–7.00 *p.m.* *Evening session.*
Motion: "That.."
Chairman: —.
Speakers: Proposer, —.
Seconder, —.

Sunday, 7th March

2.30–4.00 *p.m.* *Afternoon session.*
To consider the suggestion: "That..."
Chairman: —.
Speaker: —.

5.00–6.00 *p.m.* *Open session.*
Questions and suggestions to be handed to the Secretary in writing before 4.00 p.m.
Chairman: Sir William —, J.P., F.R.A.C.

6.30–7.00 *p.m.* *Closing session.*
Summing up by Sir William –, J.P., F.R.A.C.

Each session can have its own timetable, which can either be incorporated in the above, printed separately or merely announced by the chairman. The agenda will be circulated to all those attending the conference.

Rules

There are no set rules for conferences; the committee will draw up any it may consider necessary to meet the circumstances, unless they are already incorporated in the Standing Orders for the organisation, which is the case in many national societies, which hold regular conferences.

Rules should be few and simple. It is not possible to give an example that will meet all circumstances, but the following may be some guide:

1. No motion can be considered if it has not previously been submitted to the committee in writing.
2. The mover of a motion may speak to his motion for not more than ten minutes. The seconder may speak for not more than five minutes.
3. No other member may speak for more than five minutes and no one may speak more than once on any one motion or amendment, except the mover.
4. Amendments must be submitted to the chairman in writing, with the name of the proposer and seconder.
5. The mover of an amendment may speak for not more than five minutes.
6. The timetable must be strictly followed.
7. Delegates are requested to be punctual and will not be admitted to the hall while anyone is speaking.
8. Questions must be brief and put through the chair. The questioner should give his name on rising.
9. The chairman's ruling on matters of procedure is final.

Chairmen

At a big conference, it is advisable to have more than one chairman. It is too tiring for any one person to chair every session, and it is good for the audience to have a change of personality. The chairmen of the different sessions should be *thoroughly* conversant with the subjects to be dealt with, and this is beyond the powers of any one individual.

The chairman-in-chief will open and close the conference

and will deal with the open session, if there is one. He may chair other sessions and, in any case, will be available if required.

Chairing a conference is not easy and not to be lightly undertaken by the inexperienced. It requires an exact mind, a wide knowledge of the work of the organisation concerned, and absolute familiarity with the technique of dealing with motions and amendments.

Speakers

If the subject is a technical one, it is sometimes considered desirable to have a speaker in addition to the proposer and seconder of a motion. If so, he should be an expert on the topic under discussion, able to put over fact rather than personal opinion, and competent to answer questions.

He should not speak until after the proposer and seconder of the motion, must confine himself to the technicalities of the subject, and not speak against the motion. There have been occasions when the parent-body, not liking a motion introduced by a branch, has put up an expert speaker with the definite intention of getting the motion defeated. For anyone to speak against a motion in debate is, of course, permissible; but organised opposition from the platform, through an experienced speaker, is taking an unfair advantage of the delegates.

When subjects have been thoroughly thrashed out in the branches and the delegates are well versed in them, such additional speakers should be unnecessary.

Delegates

Information regarding delegates, fees, accommodation and so forth, should, if possible, be sent to the branches with the initial notice of the conference, as this enables them to make their plans. Final instructions can follow later with the agenda, and may be sent direct to the delegates, though it is always wise to let the branch secretary have a copy, in case of emergency.

The number of delegates allowed from each branch will depend upon circumstances. When possible, invite at least two; it is more pleasant for them and makes for greater accuracy in stating the views of the branch and reporting back to the members afterwards. Delegates must be appointed by the branch; they should be thoroughly familiar with the opinions of the people they represent and capable of putting those views before the conference. They should be given power to use their discretion in voting, to express as closely as possible the views held by their branch.

As a precaution against unauthorised persons gaining admittance to the conference, it is wise to provide each delegate with credentials. These can be sent with the final agenda, and may be slips attached to it, or they can take the form of cards bearing the official stamp of the organisation and the names of the delegates and their branches. No one should be admitted without the necessary authorisation, which can be checked at the door with the official list.

Media

If reporters and cameras are to be present, they should be dealt with in the same way as at a public meeting. Whether their presence is desirable or not is a matter of individual choice; but it should be borne in mind that it is impossible for a whole conference to be reported in detail, and the points selected by the Press and television may not be those the organisation wish emphasizing. The presence of reporters and cameras does have a withering effect on the eloquence of some delegates, especially those with little experience.

The Hall

The suggestions made in Chapter 2 apply equally to a conference, with one or two adjustments.

It is advisable to have a rostrum – or raised desk – for the use of delegates wishing to speak. This should be to one side of the platform; but, if below it, slightly raised from floor level so that the speaker can be seen by everyone. The desk is essential so that the speaker may have his notes easily accessible. A rostrum situated below the platform is often preferred by delegates, as ascending a platform imposes considerable nerve strain. In a large hall, this should be fitted with a microphone.

If possible, a system of electric signs (on the principle of traffic lights) fitted to the rostrum and connected with the chairman's table is useful. Green: go ahead; Amber: two minutes to go; Red: stop, time up. These are less disconcerting to the delegates than a bell, which is heard by everyone.

Many delegates also like to have a table for writing and to hold their papers. This should be provided if possible as physical comfort makes for better concentration. Endeavour to arrange the tables so that everyone looks towards the platform without having to perform a contortionist act, though this is sometimes unavoidable if space is limited.

There should be a small room available to the committee and officials only; they will require somewhere to foregather or to hold an emergency meeting if necessary.

Stewards and door-keepers will be required as for a public meeting, and the seating must be divided into blocks to enable the votes to be counted accurately.

The Platform

As in the hall, plenty of table space should be provided. The number of people on the platform will vary considerably according to the session, and all will wish to write easily. The chairman will, of course, sit in the centre, with the speaker on his right and the secretary on his left. At a conference, the secretary's services are in constant demand. There should be an assistant detailed to take the minutes, as the secretary will not be free to do so.

The chairman should be supplied with a proper gavel and a hard bit of wood to bang it on loudly.

Procedure

It is usual for all officers and members of the committee to be on the platform for the opening and closing sessions.

Promptly on time, the chairman will bang the gavel, call on the secretary to read the convening notice, and will then declare the conference open. Following this, he will:

1. Make a short speech, giving the reasons and objects of the conference.

2. Read the rules governing the conference.
3. Read the agenda.
4. Ask if anyone has any questions to raise on procedure; and if so, he will deal with them.
5. Call on the secretary to read any special announcements.

This should not take more than ten to fifteen minutes.

He will then either open the first session himself, or hand over to the appropriate chairman.

Procedure for a Session. The agenda for a single session will probably be as follows:

Morning Session: Saturday, 6th March

11.00 a.m.	Chairman's opening remarks.
11.05 "	Motion proposed by Mr. Robinson.
11.15 "	Motion seconded by Miss Thomas.
11.20 "	Questions
11.45 "	Discussion and amendments.
12.45 "	Motion put to meeting.
12.55 "	Close of session.

If the agenda has not been circulated to the delegates, it should be read by the chairman. He should draw attention to the time allowed for questions and discussion, and make it quite clear that he intends to keep to the timetable. He will then introduce the speakers, read the motion, and call upon the speakers.

Speakers: The chairman will first call upon the proposer and seconder of the motion to speak. If there are additional speakers, they will follow. It is possible that there may be no definite motion but merely a subject for discussion; and in this case the speaker will be called upon immediately.

As has already been stated, speakers at a conference should make their appeal to reason rather than to emotion. They should be brief, factual and avoid personal opinion; their function is to inform rather than to sway the audience, and their statements must be accurate. The expert on his own subject does not find this difficult – except, perhaps, the condition of brevity! The most effective speakers at conferences are those who outline their main points immediately, then proceed to elaborate them.

Question Time: The chairman will now call for questions as at a public meeting.

The purpose of question time, as distinct from the discussion period, is to permit delegates to gain as much information as possible on points about which they, or their branch, may not be fully informed. It is usual for questions to be answered by the speaker, but where a particular query is outside his range, the chairman may call upon anyone else he considers competent to answer.

Inquirers must be dealt with in turn, and the chairman must insist on questions only; observations and expressions of opinion must be firmly deferred until discussion time. There are usually more questions than time allows, so no one should be allowed a second query until all have had their turn.

It is unnecessary for questioners to use the rostrum, as time is wasted getting to and fro, but those wishing to speak during discussion time should do so, or use a roving microphone if available.

Discussion. When time has expired or there are no more questions, the chairman will throw the motion open for discussion and amendment. He will call upon the proposer and seconder of each previously submitted amendment in turn until all have been dealt with.

Many big conferences will not permit the consideration of any amendments not previously submitted in writing. This rule may be waived by the consent of the conference, but this should only be permitted under special circumstances, or the business might drag on interminably.

Anyone has the right to speak for or against an amendment if he can catch the chairman's eye, but as there is usually no dearth of speakers, the rule governing the number of delegates and the length of time each may speak must be strictly enforced; only the proposer of a motion or amendment has the right to speak a second time – immediately before his motion is put to the vote.

The chairman needs to keep a watchful eye on the clock, so that too much time is not spent on the earlier points, and the remainder rushed through without adequate consideration.

Taking the Vote. In accordance with the rules of debate (see Chapter 3), the amendments will be put to the vote in turn, followed by the amended motion.

The most usual method of voting is by a show of hands, though for exceptionally serious issues, or for a personal question, a ballot may be taken. When the former method is adopted, the chairman will call for "Those in favour"; and when they have been counted, "Those against". This is all too frequently omitted – which is entirely out of order. The tellers will carefully count the votes in their sections and report to the platform.

Close of Session. It is not necessary to have formal votes of thanks at the end of a session; these are usually reserved until the final gathering of the conference. The chairman should, however, thank the speakers and close the session formally, as at a public meeting.

Open Session

Time permitting, it is a good plan to have an Open Session at the end of the conference, when ideas and suggestions on matters (usually small) not included in the agenda can be raised. This is useful in giving delegates an opportunity to air views, voice complaints and gain information.

At a large meeting, the chairman will previously have asked for questions or suggestions in writing. These he will take in turn, giving the delegate responsible the opportunity to enlarge on the subject if he so wishes.

It is wise to have as many experts as possible on the platform for this session as the queries may be many and varied!

Any constructive suggestions, if approved by the conference, should be sent to the executive committee for their consideration.

Closing Session

As at the Opening Session, the officials and committee should be present for the final gathering.

The chairman should give a short summing up of the work of the conference and thank the delegates, committee and all who have helped to make it a success.

A formal vote of thanks to the chairman and to those who presided at other sessions can be moved as soon as he has concluded. This will be arranged by the committee and the proposer and seconder will proceed without being called upon by the chairman. The motion is not put to the meeting in the usual way, so agreement is taken for granted and applause started as soon as the seconder has finished. A seconder is not, however, essential under these conditions.

The chairman will then reply, and close the conference.

INFORMAL CONFERENCES

To this point we have dealt chiefly with the large formal conference, to which each branch sends delegates who have been instructed in the views of the members on definite subjects. Such convocations are of necessity run on formal lines and adhere to a pre-determined and carefully timed agenda, which limits scope for discussion and argument.

The informal conference is a smaller and less cut-and-dried affair and can be dealt with by any reasonably competent chairman. It will most probably be an afternoon meeting, whereas a big conference may last several days. Instead of appointed delegates, all the members concerned will be invited and discussion will not be confined within such strict limits.

The purpose of this type of conference is to ascertain the opinions of *individual members* on the subjects under review, and almost invariably precedes the formal convention.

The subjects for discussion may have come from the headquarters of the organisation; a branch may wish to voice a grievance or send some suggestion to the parent-body; or it may be only a local matter. Whichever it is, the opinions expressed at the meeting must be put into a clearly and properly-worded motion, to be forwarded subsequently to the appropriate committee. A conference merely makes suggestions and recommendations; it has no power to put these into effect.

Conferences are frequently called by one section of an organisation, such as the Education or the Sports Committee. Under these circumstances, only members interested in that particular activity would attend.

Procedure

The procedure for a small conference is similar to that for a single session at a full-scale one.

If the subjects for discussion have emanated from an outside source, it will probably be necessary to have a speaker to put the facts before the members, but this is usually unnecessary on purely domestic business.

There must be a time limit to discussion, but the rule governing the number of times members are permitted to speak may be relaxed if there are signs of nervousness, as too many rules tend to frighten the beginner. Questions will be intermingled with expressions of opinion, and the chairman may have to answer these or call on other members to do so.

If the business before the meeting is not already worded in the form of a motion, the chairman should make a few notes on any points which in his view require consideration, and incorporate these into his opening remarks.

Suppose that the community concerned is a local branch of a nationwide social organisation which has called a conference to discuss the following:

1. A motion received from its headquarters "That this … organisation should apply for affiliation with the International Federation of …"
2. To consider the advisability of obtaining larger premises to enable the Branch to widen the scope of its activities.

As it is possible that no one in the branch knows much about the proposed affiliation, it is most likely a speaker has been invited to explain what it means, why it is recommended and its effects. The procedure will then follow that given in the previous chapter.

The second type of procedure, dealing with a purely local matter, would not call for a special speaker. The formally-worded motion would develop as a result of discussion, and the wise chairman should note down a few points to ensure that the subject is dealt with from every angle, e.g.:

1. Are larger premises really necessary?
2. What type is required – house, hall, wooden hut, etc.?

3. Do we want any land with it for recreation, allotments, etc.?
4. Has anyone any premises in mind?
5. How are they to be financed – bought, rented?
6. How is the money to be raised?
7. Who is going to be responsible?
8. Are any restrictions to be placed on their use?

Framing Motions from Discussion

On concluding his opening remarks, the chairman will take the first point, e.g. "Now let us consider whether we really do need larger premises. Would any member like to say anything on this point?" Discussion will then follow. When the chairman considers that all who wish to do so have expressed their opinions or that enough time has been spent on this point, he will ask if anyone would care to propose a motion that larger premises are necessary. If a member does so, the wording must be carefully written down, read to the conference and then seconded. If no definite motion is put forward, the chairman or secretary must draft one, read it to the meeting and call for a proposer and seconder, or ask members by name to do so.

The conference, having now decided that it does want new premises, will go on to discuss details as to the type of building, whether it should have land, etc. These details will be added to the original motion in the form of amendments (each proposed and seconded) after being dealt with in a similar manner to the original motion. The amendments and finally the amended motion will then be put to the vote as explained in Chapter 3. The final resolution, which incorporates all the chairman's points, passed as amendments, would probably read as follows: "That this conference considers larger premises are essential and that a suitable house be purchased, with sufficient land for recreational purposes; the cost to be defrayed by the members and a mortgage and the management placed in the hands of a standing committee to be appointed."

Another way of dealing with such a question is to discuss the whole subject, then to draw up an omnibus motion incorporating all the ideas, instead of building it up, bit by bit, by means of amendments. This is quicker and more informal, but requires an extremely clear-headed chairman or some important matter will be omitted.

The great secret in dealing with this type of conference is to write down points as they occur. It appears simple to remember all the suggestions, but is not so in fact, especially for the less experienced chairman.

Discussion should not be allowed to drag on. As soon as new ideas and suggestions cease to be forthcoming and members begin repeating themselves, make the conference come to some decision or pass on to the next item. This can be done by the chairman or by a member moving a closure (page 56). There comes a time in any discussion when the mind ceases to function really clearly and becomes incapable of producing any new thought; as soon as this happens, further talk is waste of time and the chairman should judge when the moment has arrived to close the subject. If he considers the members have enough material to enable them to make their decision, he should call for the motion or amendment; if he feels they are still insufficiently informed, he should defer the matter pending further information, and pass on to the next item. Whichever alternative is adopted, the discussion should be kept active.

5

STARTING A NEW ORGANISATION

When the founding of a new organisation or society is contemplated, it is as well to be quite clear on three points:

1. What is a society?
2. What is its purpose?
3. What is its composition?

1. A society or organisation is a group of people who band themselves together for some specific purpose. It may be composed of a few members or many thousands, of international standing or purely local, but all within its membership are joined for the purpose of furthering its aims.

2. These aims may be religious, political, educational, commercial, recreational or purely social, and are usually a combination of several. Whatever the object for which the society is formed, it must be clearly stated in the Constitution.

3. Whether large or small, the composition of a society is basically the same. It consists of officers, committee and ordinary members. In a large organisation, there are innumerable branches and sections, but each will repeat this structure: thus the local branch of any big society is almost identical in construction with its headquarters and governed by the same set of rules – or Standing Orders.

Conditions may indicate the need for a new society or branch of an established one, which will require the action of someone with imagination and initiative to co-ordinate the feeling of the community. When this occurs, the first thing is to prepare the ground by enlisting the support of influential members of the community and then to call a meeting to discuss the project.

Inaugural Meeting

This will be held either in a public room or a private house – most probably the latter – and all those who may be interested will be invited.

The first business will be to elect a chairman for the meeting and members are likely to propose the inaugurator of the scheme, which is often wise, as it is a compliment. On the other hand, it might be better to choose an experienced chairman, and to leave the enthusiastic inaugurator free to speak and explain his ideas. A temporary secretary should be also appointed to take the minutes.

If the purpose of the meeting is to decide whether or not to start a branch of some well-known organisation, it is most likely that a speaker will have been obtained from headquarters, in which case the inaugurator could well take the chair.

The business before the meeting will be considerable. It has to decide, first, whether it wants the society or not; and, if it does, it must set up the machinery for running it.

Thc quickest way to approach the first question is to have the scheme embodied in a motion, which can be read to the meeting by the chairman, e.g. *That this meeting considers a Youth Club should be formed for the purposes of education and recreation, as it views with alarm the increase of petty delinquency among young people.*

This motion will be used by the speaker as the basis of his talk, which should be confined to explaining the need for a Youth Centre, the benefits to be derived from it, and an outline of its management.

After the talk, members should be given an opportunity for questions and discussion, but these should, at this stage, be confined to whether or not the Youth Club shall be formed, as questions relating to its construction and management need not be considered until the motion has been passed. If any alteration to the motion is necessary, it will be done by amending it in the usual way.

When the motion forming the Club has been passed, the next step is to decide its Constitution and Rules. To do this in detail at a fair-sized meeting is almost impossible, so the alternative is for the conveners of the meeting to have a set ready drafted to submit to members. "To draft in haste is to repent at leisure", however, and a more satisfactory set of rules is likely to result from discussion.

Possibly the most satisfactory way is to meet, pass the resolution forming the society, then to appoint a small drafting committee of two or three to draw up the Constitution and Rules; and finally to adjourn the meeting for a week or so to give this committee time to do their job. When members reassemble, they will pass the Constitution and Rules, either as they stand or after amendment, then complete the inauguration by electing officers and committee for the first period.

Drafting the Constitution and Rules

The Constitution is the framework of the society and must embody a clear statement of its objects.

The Rules – or Standing Orders – give the methods by which these objects may be achieved.

Where the new society is to be a branch of an existing organisation, its constitution and Standing Orders will naturally conform to those already laid down by the organisation, with possible minor adaptations to suit local conditions. When it is an entirely new organisation, it will form its own from the outset.

The Constitution of any organisation should be clearly worded and as simple as possible in the initial stage, to leave room for additions if these are found to be necessary as the society develops. The three essential points it must include are: the name of the society, the number of executive officers and committee members, and the purpose for which the society is founded, e.g.:

That this society shall be called "The G— Youth Club."

That this society shall consist of President, Chairman, Hon. Secretary, Hon. Treasurer and Committee not exceeding ... in number, in addition to ordinary members.

That the object of the society shall be to provide recreation and education for those under eighteen years of age.

In some societies, the President is always the chairman, but it is more usual to have a President (who is often a figure-head) and a chairman and vice-chairman, who are elected annually.

It will also be noted that the objects of the society are unfettered by any restrictions as to type of recreation and education, the area in which members must reside, and so on. The Constitution must always be strictly adhered to; therefore, the wider its terms, the easier it is for the society to expand.

To give a sample set of rules is quite impossible, as they are purely individual to the body concerned. Rule-making is not easy. The commonest mistake is to make too many in an effort to cover every eventuality. It is not possible to see *exactly* how a new society will develop, so do not hamper it at the outset with too many restrictions; they will only stultify growth or be disregarded, which is a source of weakness. Rules should be a guide only, to help the society attain its objects with the maximum efficiency, therefore their aim should be to direct, and flexibility will leave scope for the good sense and initiative of the officials and members.

Rules fall mainly into two sections: those dealing with the procedure for meetings and those directly affecting members.

Rules of procedure need not be very complicated, and for a small, new society, the simpler the better. Additions can always be made as the work develops. A few necessary points of procedure are:

1. The maximum and minimum number of members on the committee.
2. The number necessary for a quorum.
3. How frequently the committee must meet.
4. How voting is to be carried out.
5. The period of office for officers and committee members.
6. When and how they are to be elected.
7. Rules for filling sudden vacancies on the committee and co-opting.
8. Rules governing debate and so on.

Those directly affecting members might be:

1. Conditions of membership.
2. Amount of subscription.
3. Rules governing activities.

When the Constitution and Rules have been passed, every member must receive a copy.

Election of Officers and Committee

After the Constitution and Standing Orders have been dealt with, the next business is to *appoint* provisional officers and committee members as it is better if they are not *elected* until the first annual general meeting. Some societies elect their officers and committee straight away, but at this point, when there are not many members, it is not a good plan as it does not allow for the opinions of members who are not yet enrolled, and it is often difficult to assess the suitability of nominees at such an early stage.

No one should be nominated for election (or appointment) to any office unless he has first been asked if he is willing to stand; neglect of this commonsense precaution causes waste of time and often embarrasses the nominee if he is elected when he does not wish to be.

The usual procedure is to elect the officers first, then the committee. The post of President should be dealt with first (if appropriate), then that of chairman. Each candidate will need a proposer and seconder, and it is best to insist on receiving nominations *in writing* before the meeting. Candidates should also signify that they consent to stand.

Voting could be done by a show of hands, but this is rather public and can lead to problems later. It is safer to vote by ballot where a post is contested. This of course means that ballot papers need to be prepared (hence the need for advance notice of nominations). Scrutineers and tellers will have to be appointed to issue and collect back the voting papers, and count them.

The secretary and treasurer will be dealt with similarly and so on to the committee. This procedure is the same: each suggested member must be proposed and seconded, and all names must be in before the voting starts. It is a good plan to have more nominations than seats, to allow for selection; but this happy state of affairs seldom occurs and if there is a difficulty in filling places, it is better to have a vacancy than to put in someone unsuitable, as it is invariably the least efficient people who are difficult to remove later, when their places may be wanted for some particularly good candidates.

Contested committee elections are also best dealt with by ballot. If done by a show of hands it can be difficult to ensure that members do not exceed their vote allocation. Also, where there are more nominations than seats, it can be embarrassing to watch the exclusion of known individuals. A ballot solves these difficulties, although it does need more preparation. The ballot papers should be pre-printed, and state clearly the maximum number of candidates to vote for.

There is another method of electing officers which is adopted by some organisations. The committee is elected first, then retires and elects the officers from amongst its own members. Should the new society be a branch of an established body, it must follow the method laid down in the rules of that organisation, otherwise the first system is the more usual and possibly the better, as it gives the members more control over the appointment.

General Meetings

Any meeting at which the ordinary members of an organisation are present is called a General Meeting, and no major business – such as an alteration to the Constitution or Rules, or the undertaking of any wide new activities – may be transacted without such a meeting being called to inform the members and obtain their consent to the project.

Every organisation holds a general meeting once a year to receive business reports, elect officers and committee, and transact routine business for the year. This is called The Annual General Meeting.

Many societies hold meetings of all the members at stated invervals, say once a month. These are Ordinary General Meetings and may be concerned with the activities of the society rather than its policy or business.

It may, however, be necessary to call a special meeting at any time to decide some issue of major importance which cannot wait until the next general meeting. These are called Extraordinary General Meetings.

Registering a New Society

All charitable societies, that is, those which receive money from the public, must, by law, be registered with the Charity Commission. The Commission produce many good booklets, some of which set out the advantages and responsibilities of running a charity, and give details of how to register a Charity with the Commissioners. They are happy to give advice to anyone considering setting up a charitable society.

When you apply to the Charity Commission to register your society you will receive a questionnaire to fill in with which you will have to return two copies of your draft governing document. If your society is accepted it will eventually be entered in the Central Register of Charities, copies of which are held at the Charity Commission's offices.

6

COMMITTEES AND COMMITTEE MEETINGS

COMMITTEES

A committee is a specified number of people to whom the members of an organisation *commit* the management of the society. It will comprise a chairman, a secretary and a definite number of members; and all committees are similarly constituted.

There are four types of committee (listed below), and the beginner should understand the functions of each and its place in the general constitution of a society.

1. The Exccutive Committee or Council – elected at the Annual General Meeting.
2. Standing Committees – appointed by the Executive Committee.
3. *Ad hoc* or Sub-Committees – appointed by any committee.
4. Joint Committees – appointed by two or more societies.

The Executive Committee

This is the leading committee in any organisation. It is elected by the members to administer the society and is responsible to them. As the name implies, it is given very wide executive powers.

Members of this committee are elected individually at the annual general meeting and its officers will consist of a chairman, vice-chairman, secretary and treasurer. Ex-officio officers may also attend (see Chapter 8). Their term of office will be laid down in the Standing Orders and is usually one year, though many societies have a three-year rota (that is, one-third of the members retire each year), which encourages the introduction of new members while ensuring continuity.

The duties of this committee are many. It is responsible for the entire management of the organisation and has extensive freedom of action. Though technically responsible to the members, it must frequently act on its own initiative if the work is to go ahead. In practice, the larger the organisation, the more powerful the executive body, as it is more difficult to obtain the views of the ordinary members; but in no organisation can any vital legislation be put into effect without the consent of the members, and any change in rules and policy must *always* be approved by them.

A small society will probably need only one permanent committee to manage its affairs, but a large organisation may have to decentralise its work and will, therefore, have to appoint assistant committees; for example, one of the following:

Standing Committees

These are committees appointed by the executive body to deal with separate sections of the work – such as finance, education, welfare, public relations and so on. As the name implies, they are permanent committees, whose members are appointed at intervals, usually every year, by the parent body.

Their scope is confined to their own particular section and their duties are advisory. They may be given limited executive powers but usually all their actions must first receive sanction from the Executive Committee, as it is they who are held responsible by the members.

Usually the chairman of a Standing Committee is a member of the executive body and can make his report in the ordinary course of attending the meeting. If not, he is usually invited to attend their meeting at a given time, for the purpose of giving his report and answering any questions about it, but leaves as soon as his business is over.

Sub-Committees

To decentralise still further, it is sometimes necessary for Standing Committees to sub-divide. These sub-committees are small, specialised, purely advisory bodies who automatically cease to exist when the appointing committee goes out of office.

Ad Hoc Committees

These are committees appointed for a special purpose. The chairman is usually a member of the appointing committee. It may be composed of members of the appointing body and frequently co-opts outside experts on the matter under review. It should be small – not more than five or six – as this makes for speed and ease in planning. Its functions are advisory though the parent body may grant it certain executive powers. It has no definite term of office, but stays in being until the work for which it was appointed is finished.

Joint Committees

These are set up by two or more societies dealing with a similar problem and may be a Standing Committee with a permanent status or an *ad hoc* committee appointed for a special purpose only.

Appointments to such committees will usually be made by the Executive Committees of the societies concerned, and their function is to co-ordinate the working of the various organisations and so prevent needless overlapping and friction.

The management of an organisation by various committees is a thoroughly democratic system. As the following illustration shows, the ordinary members have the control if they exercise it constitutionally, as the various committees are brought into existence by the will of the members and are ultimately responsible to them, as shown in the following table:

ANNUAL GENERAL MEETING
at which the ordinary members of the society elect the

EXECUTIVE COMMITTEE
which, in turn, appoints the necessary

STANDING COMMITTEES
These are advisory and may not take action without consent of the

EXECUTIVE COMMITTEE
which is responsible to, and may not take major action without the consent of the

ANNUAL GENERAL MEETING
which is composed of ordinary members.

Note: – Any of the above can appoint a sub-committee, which is responsible to the body which appointed it and no one else.

COMMITTEE MEETINGS

All committee meetings, of whatever size or type, are conducted upon similar lines, and any variation which may occur is usually a matter of chairmanship.

Convening

When permanent committees have a definite day each week or month upon which meetings are held, previous notice is not necessary, but where this is not the case, an announcement of the meeting must be sent to all the members *at least* a week before the date fixed; longer if possible.

Meetings must be convened *in writing;* verbal intimations are not adequate, being the cause of many inaccuracies and mistakes; and a written notice must be sent to every member, even though it is known that one or two among the number will be unable to attend. Some societies have convening notices printed, with blanks left for date, time and place of meeting. The same can be achieved with a word processor. This is an excellent plan as it is easy for the secretary to send such notices, which are usually on the following lines:

(ADDRESS AND
PHONE NO.)

G— YOUTH CLUB

A meeting of the Executive Committee will be held at 3 p.m. on Thursday, the 18th January, in the Youth Centre, 13 High Street. Kindly notify the secretary if you cannot attend.

JACK JONES
(Secretary).

If the agenda is ready, it can be added below the convening notice, but if not, notices of the meeting should not be held up on this account, as agendas can follow later.

Agenda

This is the programme of the business to be discussed and a copy must reach every member *at least* twenty-four hours before the meeting. Small societies sometimes omit this – considering it adequate if a copy is on the table at the meeting – which is entirely out of order as the whole purpose of the agenda paper is to give members time to consider the business under review and possibly consult those they may represent.

Agendas are all similar in construction and the following is a typical example:

MEETING OF THE G— YOUTH CLUB
EXECUTIVE COMMITTEE
the 18th January (year)

AGENDA

1. Apologies for absence.
2. Minutes of the last meeting.
3. Business arising out of the minutes.
4. Correspondence.
5. To receive reports from:
   Education Committee
   Finance Committee
6. To consider...
7. ...
8. Any other business.
9. Date and time of next meeting.

Chairmanship

Chairing a committee requires tact, patience and a sound knowledge of the business before the meeting. It is essential that the chairman and secretary work in close co-operation. The chairman must be conversant with the agenda and not rely on the secretary to "pull him through" – a deplorable state of affairs all too frequently encountered in the small society where the chairman has been selected on account of his position rather than for any ability or interest he may have in the Society.

In a small committee, too much formality is undesirable and some of the rules of debate can be relaxed. It is, however, essential that the chairman keep control of the meeting and he will be wise to check all irrelevant interruption and insist that everyone addresses the chair. If he feels that free conversation on any subject will be beneficial, it is a good plan to throw the matter open to general discussion rather than pretend to ignore the unofficial talk taking place, and the writers of this book frequently adopt this plan with excellent results. Having put the matter before the meeting, the chairman can say, "I think you may like to talk this over amongst yourselves, so we will have ten minutes' free discussion." Metaphorically, the mace is put under the table and everyone is at liberty to speak directly to anyone else. At the end of the appointed time, the chairman will call the members back to order and the meeting will proceed on more formal lines.

In an effort to be informal, some chairmen consider the passing of formal motions out of place in the small committee, and allow measures to be voted upon without first being correctly worded. This is a mistake and can lead to a lot of argument later. The whole point of a motion is to crystallise the ideas and opinions of the meeting into a straightforward, concise sentence, about which there can be no subsequent misunderstanding, and to do this is surely commonsense, not pedantry. Another snare is for the lazy committee to leave the wording of the resolution to the chairman or secretary, after passing the idea in substance, on the grounds that "you know what we mean". This should never be permitted or trouble is sure to follow, as someone is certain to question the interpretation of "what we mean".

It is a common fallacy that the inexperienced committee should not be run on formal lines for fear of discouraging the members. On the contrary, provided the procedure is enforced with tact and patience (and a sense of humour), members prefer some formality: it engenders a feeling of competence and they quickly learn to appreciate its time-saving effect. It should also be remembered that the small committee is the training ground of both officers and members for possible bigger things.

Technically, everything discussed in committee is confidential. It is, of course, not always practicable to enforce this, but circumstances may make it advisable for the chairman to warn members against any breach of confidence.

Procedure

The procedure for committee meetings is the same for all types of committee. The agenda must be strictly adhered to and no other business can be introduced, or the order be altered, without the consent of members.

No meeting can be held unless there is a *quorum,* that is, a minimum number of members who must be present before business can be transacted. The number will be laid down in the Standing Orders and is usually not less than one-third of the total number of committee members, excluding officers, or in the case of a very small committee, not less than three members. This is obviously a wise and necessary precaution against inadequate representation and consequent hole-and-corner legislation.

Punctuality should be encouraged. If the meeting begins strictly on time, members will quickly realise that slackness is not to be tolerated; there are few things more irritating to the busy person than waiting for the unpunctual one. Should there not be a quorum (which only rarely occurs), the chairman should wait five or ten minutes only, then, if there are still insufficient members, dismiss the meeting.

It is permissible for the chairman to remain seated in committee, and it is not usually necessary for members to stand when addressing the chair, though it is often desirable and should be enforced in a large or obstreperous meeting.

Meeting Opened and Apologies for Absence. Strictly at the appointed time, the chairman will open the meeting and either read the names of those who have apologised for absence or ask the secretary to do so. Letters should not be read as this is usually unnecessary, and if they contain matters of interest to members, should come under Correspondence or the item on the agenda to which they refer.

Minutes of the Last Meeting. If the minutes have been circulated to members with the agenda, there is no need to read them out and the chairman will say, "You have read the minutes of the last meeting; is it your pleasure that I sign them as correct?" If any member wishes to question the accuracy of the minutes as a record of what took place at the last meeting, he must say so at once before they are signed. If the majority agree with his correction, the alteration must be made to the minute in question *in ink* and initialled by the chairman. When members are satisfied that they are correct, they will signify their approval by a show of hands and the chairman will sign and date the minute book in ink. If the minutes are handwritten, only the last page need be signed, but if typed or photocopied, his signature or initials must appear on every page.

Business Arising out of the Minutes. This item of the agenda can be a snare for the unwary chairman. The business is merely a report of action taken as a result of decisions made at the last meeting, for the purpose of bringing the committee up to date. For example: at the last meeting it was decided to hold a fête and the secretary (or possibly some other committee member) was requested to:

1. Ask Mr. B— for the use of his field.
2. Invite Sir W— B— to open the fête.
3. Engage the local band
4. Obtain estimates for catering.

Under "Business Arising", the secretary will be asked to report the result of his inquiries. These may be:

1. Mr. B— will grant the use of his field.
2. Sir W— B— regrets he is unable to open the fête.
3. The band has been engaged.
4. Estimates have been submitted for catering.

The Committee will then proceed to consider item no. 2 and suggest alternative people to be asked to open the fête. Item 4 will then be discussed and the estimates considered. It is very easy for discussion to wander from the points at issue and the chairman must be careful to keep it relevant or time is wasted.

Correspondence. This item is to allow the reading and discussion of letters which are not relevant to any of the subjects on the agenda. Any letters concerning items of business already on the agenda will be dealt with under the appropriate heading.

Reports. In an organisation having Standing Committees, the reports from each will be given by its chairman or some other appointed representative. Any recommendations made to the parent body by such a committee should be in the form of resolutions, to ensure accuracy and clarity, and these will be considered and either approved, turned down or referred back for further consideration. Reports from sub-committees and joint committees will be dealt with similarly by the body appointing them.

In a small society, there will be few or no reports, though it is usual to have a report from the treasurer regarding the financial position.

Other Items. The committee will now deal in turn with the various items of new business. These may be in the form of resolutions sent from other bodies, motions submitted by members, or merely informal suggestions for consideration. If the latter, the matter will require discussing and, if it calls for a definite decision, drafting into a properly worded motion and a vote taken. Suggestions as to the method of doing this are given in Chapter 4 under "Informal Conferences".

Any Other Business. This item can be another trap for the inexperienced chairman. Its purpose is to give members an opportunity to raise matters of minor importance which have not been included in the agenda, but it is sometimes used to rush through important measures without adequate consideration.

Being always at the end of the agenda, members with other commitments may have left, thinking the real business concluded, which results in a much reduced meeting. Under these conditions, it is not uncommon for the less co-operative minority of a committee to bring forward some important suggestion, in an attempt to get it passed by the remaining members, who are probably tired, anxious to leave and not in a fit state to put up any considered opposition, as might be the case if they had notice of the scheme.

It can also happen that some suggestion introduced quite

innocently may develop into a subject of major importance, and the chairman must be awake to this danger.

No major matter should ever be put to the vote under "Any Other Business". If he thinks fit, the chairman may allow some discussion; then he should firmly defer the subject, to be brought forward on the next agenda – thus giving adequate warning to all; and it is only fair to absent members.

Next Meeting. If the committee meets regularly, there is no need to include this item. If meetings are irregular, it is helpful to fix the date of the next meeting, but this does not obviate the necessity for sending out convening notices.

Meeting Closed. It is essential that the meeting be closed as soon as the agenda is completed. Sometimes further discussion breaks out and, although the meeting is really over, the secretary – and often the members too – is not quite sure whether such discussions should be recorded or not; whereas if the meeting has been finally declared at an end, any subsequent talk is "off the record".

7

ANNUAL GENERAL MEETINGS

Every society, whatever its size, must call its members together once a year for an annual general meeting. This meeting must be held within fifteen months of the previous one and the account books of the organisation must be available for any member who may wish to inspect them. Only members have this right.

The purpose of this meeting is to receive a report of the work of the past year, to pass the accounts, to plan for the year ahead by electing the Executive officers and committee members and to approve suggestions put forward regarding future policy and activities.

In a small society, every member will be invited to the annual general meeting; but when the organisation is a national one, it is obviously impossible for every member to attend one central meeting except by representation. In such cases, each branch holds its own annual general meeting, which every member is entitled to attend. The branch report is then sent to the county or area, which in turn holds its annual meeting, to which as many members as possible are invited from each branch. The county or area report, incorporating the branch reports, is then sent to the headquarters, where a general report is compiled on behalf of the whole organisation, and is presented at its annual general meeting, to which representatives from the counties or areas are invited.

Whether the meeting is held by a small branch or by the national headquarters, the purpose and procedure are identical.

Agenda

The agenda for an annual general meeting can usually go out with the invitations, as there are unlikely to be any last-minute additions necessary. Agendas comform approximately to the following example:

THIRD ANNUAL GENERAL MEETING OF THE
G— YOUTH CLUB

AGENDA

1. Apologies for absence.
2. Minutes of the last Annual General Meeting.
3. Chairman's address.
4. To receive the annual report from:
   The Secretary.
   The Treasurer.
5. Adoption of reports:
   Moved by Mr. R—.
   Seconded by Mr. W—.
6. Election of officers and executive committee.
7. To consider the recommendation that...
8. Any other business.

Procedure

It is usual for the President to take the chair at the annual general meeting. The procedure is similar to that at a committee meeting, though there are some differences and it is not usually a difficult meeting to conduct.

Apologies for Absence. In a small society, it may be advisable to read all the names. Usually, it is sufficient to mention any absent official by name, then merely to state the number of apologies received from ordinary members. Alternatively, the whole item can be omitted.

Minutes of Previous Meeting. These are usually very short. Some organisations circulate a copy with the annual report immediately after the meeting to which they refer, in which case they need not be read at the next meeting. In many instances, the chairman considers reading minutes a year old to be a waste of time, as the present members are not necessarily those who attended last year's meeting, so he asks permission from the meeting to take them as read. Whichever method is adopted, they must be formally passed by the meeting, then signed and dated by the chairman.

There have been instances where the Executive committee has taken upon itself the passing of these minutes at its first meeting after the annual general meeting. This is out of order. If the committee likes to check up on the minutes while events are fresh in mind and make a note of any inaccuracy, it is an excellent plan, but the committee has no power officially to pass the minutes: only the meeting concerned can do that, for obvious reasons!

Address by Chairman. This is not a universal procedure, but if the chairman can give a general review of the work done during the past year, leaving facts and figures to the reports, it is more stimulating and interesting than the reading of the reports alone. Care must be taken to avoid too much repetition and overlapping with the reports.

Reports. The secretary will read his report first, followed by the treasurer and any others there may be. In some societies, each section gives its own report; but it is inadvisable to have too many or members will get restive. If there must be several, a strict time limit should be imposed.

Adoption of the Reports. When all the reports have been read, the chairman will call upon one member to move and another to second the adoption of each one. If either of these members wishes to make a short speech about the report, he is at liberty to do so, but his remarks should be brief and relevant. The chairman will then ask if any member wishes to comment on the reports, after which the motion for their adoption will be put to the vote.

The adoption of the reports cannot be moved or seconded by anyone who is not a member of the society.

This completes the first part of the business. Members have been fully informed of what has taken place during the past year, they have been given the opportunity for comment and criticism, and are now ready to pass on to planning for the year ahead.

Election of Officers and Executive Committee. If the presidency of the society is a yearly appointment and the President is offering himself for re-election, he must vacate the chair during the period of the election and hand over the office to a temporary chairman. If, however, the presidency is a long-term office or the present holder is not open to re-election, the situation does not arise.

Too often, members are confronted with a chairman who remains firmly in the chair and naïvely informs them that he is willing to stand for re-election to the office. They may be very unwilling to re-appoint him, but under these circumstances it is extremely difficult not to do so and requires more courage than most people possess.

Before embarking on the election, it is usual for the President to say a few words of thanks to the retiring chairman and/or other officers. When these officials have been efficient, it is easy to be sincere, but if they have been incapable, tiresome or merely inert, it is more difficult. Under these circumstances, it is better not to pretend all has been as it should be, as this belittles the good work of others and creates a wrong sense of values. There is usually some achievement or plan that can receive favourable mention; if not, there is certain to be some reason for the deficiency, such as ill-health, business or family troubles and so forth, which can be introduced sympathetically as a valid reason for failure.

The various methods of carrying out elections are dealt with in Chapter 8.

To Consider Recommendations. Any matter requiring ratification by the general meeting will be brought forward in the form of a resolution from the body submitting the suggestion – usually the executive committee – and will be dealt with by the ordinary procedure governing motions. There may be some amendments, but generally such motions have been thoroughly thrashed out beforehand at all levels of the organisation, so that little, if any, further alteration is necessary.

Any Other Business. This gives members an opportunity to raise matters not on the agenda. It is not often that anything very vital is brought forward, but if it is, the objection against dealing with such matters under this heading in a committee does not apply so strongly, and the subject must be thrown open to discussion and, if necessary, a decision taken. Should the measure be of a far-reaching nature, the meeting may consider it wise to defer it and either hand it over to the Executive committee to deal with or call an Extraordinary general meeting after members have had time to consider the matter; but, as the ultimate authority in the organisation and responsible to no one else, they have the right, subject to the rules, to make any decision they think fit at the annual general meeting. When the business is concluded, the meeting must be formally closed.

Some organisations invite a guest speaker to give a short talk on some aspect of the society's work. In this event, the chairman will introduce the speaker as at a public meeting and the meeting will then be conducted along those lines.

Annual Reports

Officers presenting the annual reports have a great responsibility as the knowledge of the members depends very much on the accurate compiling and interesting presentation of these reports. Annual reports should comprise an accurate, factual history of the work of the organisation during the previous year, and must be clear, logical and concise.

In practice, there are two reports prepared: the fully detailed one for the printed copy and the abbreviated and relevant edition to be read at the annual meeting. The former must give statistics and figures in full, whereas the latter should avoid too much detail but focus attention on actual achievements. It should not omit, however, to mention the less successful undertakings, so that the organisation can learn by its mistakes and a true balance of performance be obtained.

The financial report in particular should avoid giving too many figures, as these are meaningless to most people unless the statistics are actually in front of them. It is not always necessary to read the *detailed* balance-sheet as this will appear in print and in any case it is better to concentrate on analysing the financial situation. If the income has decreased or increased, explain where and why. Tell the members where activities had to be curtailed through lack of money. Explain where development is desirable and how much it would cost.

Draw attention to any good money-raising ventures. Endeavour to interest the members in finance, to show them that money is not just "one of those tiresome things" but the life-blood of any organisation. Make them realise that their subscriptions and money-raising efforts are not just dull routine but vitally necessary to the success and existence of the society.

Practice is required to read a report properly and it is well worthwhile taking trouble over this. How often have we all tried to listen to a mumbled, gabbled reading, the meaning of which we have largely lost because it was inaudible? However well written the report may be, it will fail to interest the audience if it is badly delivered.

The reader of a report should first of all make himself thoroughly conversant with its contents. Read it aloud for practice, note where pause and emphasis are advantageous and mark the script accordingly as a reminder. If possible, do not keep your eyes glued to the paper but look up from time to time to finish a sentence spontaneously. Provided the essence is accurate and the statements clear, there is no need for reports to be delivered word for word as written. Every member will eventually receive a copy of the detailed version for reference and at the meeting it is better to present it in an interesting manner than to be word perfect.

Stand easily in an upright position, with the script held well up so that it can be read without bending the head unduly. Read slowly and clearly, with due regard for punctuation. Pause at the end of each paragraph, as passing too quickly from one subject to another does not allow time for the mind to become adjusted to the new line of thought and consequently is irritating to the audience. The voice follows the eyes, so the more the reader can look at the audience the better, as this will bring him into closer contact with them.

Have the sheets of the script fastened together so that they cannot fall or be blown about. This also ensures that they do not get out of order, which is disconcerting to the nervous.

As soon as the reports have been adopted by the annual general meeting, they must be printed – or duplicated – and a copy sent to each member. Some societies have this done before the meeting, to enable members to digest the contents first. This is a good plan but financially risky as, should any alteration have to be made as a result of the meeting, it would probably necessitate a reprint; so the more usual plan is to distribute the report after the meeting.

8

ELECTION OF OFFICERS AND COMMITTEE

Both the method of electing the officers and committee members and the procedure to be followed are, or should be, given in the rules of every organisation; but, as usually only the mere outline is stated, a more detailed consideration of the alternative methods and procedure may be helpful.

Alternative Methods

1. Officers and committee members are elected for a stated period by the members of the organisation at the annual general meeting. The officers are elected individually first, followed by the committee members, either individually or en bloc.

2. The officers are not elected at the annual general meeting. Members elect the committee only, for a given period, the latter appointing the officers from amongst themselves. This enables the committee to choose its own officers without reference to the members and is the method adopted in Local Government, where the councillors are elected by the people and in turn appoint the mayor from amongst their own number.

3. Officers and committee are elected for a definite period – usually three years – and retire on a rota sytstem: one officer and a third of the committee each year. This makes for continuity of control but takes longer for undesirable elements of the committee to be eliminated. A variation of this rota system is to elect officers, especially the chairman, for one year only – a method sometimes followed in Local Government, where a third of the councillors may retire each year, though the mayor is appointed annually.

Period of Service. This will be laid down in the rules of the organisation. Unless the rota system is adopted, it is usually one year. As a safeguard against officers and committee being repeatedly re-elected (a frequent cause of "dead wood" in a society), the rules should state a limit to the time anyone may serve without a break, and some clause such as *No officer or member of a committee may offer himself for re-election more than ... consecutive times* is extremely beneficial, as it ensures the periodical introduction of new blood.

When the rota system is first introduced, the order of retirement for the first two years is usually arranged by drawing lots. After this period, it becomes automatic.

In large voluntary organisations, the office of secretary and treasurer may be salaried posts, in which case they are not elected by the members and do not have the same status and voting power as voluntary officers, who should always be distinguished by being called *honorary* – usually shortened to *Hon. Sec. or Hon. Treas.*

The President or chairman is invariably an honorary appointment, therefore the prefix is unnecessary and he is always elected to the office.

Procedure Governing Elections

Nominations for the elections should be sent to the secretary before the annual general meeting. Many organisations circulate the names to their members with the agenda, to allow time for consideration, especially if there are more nominations than places to be filled. Some organisations allow additional names to be submitted at the annual general meeting.

No one should be nominated without his consent being obtained first.

Every name nominated for the first time must be proposed, seconded and put to the vote separately.

Officers must always be voted upon separately, but the names of retiring committee members offering themselves for re-election can be proposed, seconded and voted upon en bloc. This is a great saving of time, but creates rather a delicate situation if members wish to eliminate one or two names. If previous efforts to get the persons concerned to withdraw before the meeting fail, the only way to achieve this is for a member to propose an amendment such as *With the exception of...* This must be seconded and put to the vote; and, if carried, the names are deleted. Provisional appointments should be confirmed separately and not included in members re-elected en bloc (see paragraph on Filling Vacancies later in this chapter).

Methods of Voting

There are two commonly used methods of voting at elections:

1. By a show of hands.
2. By ballot.

1. *Voting by a show of hands* is something adopted by small organisations though it should not be used where there is much competition or where there are several vacancies. It helps future harmony in an organisation if no-one knows who voted for whom!

The chairman – or temporary chairman, in the event of the chairman being one of the nominees will deal with the election of the officers in order of importance, beginning with the President or chairman. He will first read the names of those nominated for the office, with their proposers and seconders. Then each will be put to the vote in turn, on the following lines: "We have before us two names for the office of chairman: Mr. B—, proposed by Miss T- and seconded by Mr. H—; and Mrs. W—, proposed by Mr. R— and seconded by Mr. S—. Will those in favour of Mr. B— please hold up their right hands." The votes are then counted by the "tellers" and recorded. He will then put the second name, "Those in favour of Mrs. W—". These votes, too, are counted and the candidate with the most votes will be declared elected. Other officers are dealt with similarly.

If there is only one nominee, the name will be put to the vote to ratify his appointment "unopposed".

The next step will be to read out the names of committee members offering themselves for election. These will be proposed, seconded and put to the vote en bloc.

Nominations for new members to fill vacancies will now be put to the meeting individually. Should there be more names than vacancies, the chairman must remind members of this, pointing out that although there are seven nominations, there are only five vacancies: therefore they have only five votes – otherwise there may be confusion. But, in this circumstance it is safer and better to have a ballot.

To ensure impartiality, it is wise to take nominations in alphabetical order.

2. *Voting by Ballot* is a fair and sensible system, but it takes longer and requires more organisation than the previous method.

The ballot can be taken at the annual general meeting or by post beforehand. Whichever method is adopted, it is necessary to appoint some independent person as "Returning Officer", to be responsible for the proper distribution and collection of the ballot papers, to organise and oversee the counting of the votes and to check up on any defaced or incorrectly filled up ballot papers.

If the ballot is to be taken by post, voting papers must be circulated and a date fixed for their return. If voting is to be carried out at the meeting, the papers will be issued to each member on arrival.

When voting is to be done at the annual general meeting, some organisations allow absent members to name other members as their proxies. Under these circumstances, a proxy form will be issued by the Returning Officer before the meeting, which must be filled in and signed by the member absenting himself and presented by the proxy before he can obtain the necessary voting paper. Only a member of the society should be allowed to act as proxy.

Before and during a ballot, the Returning Officer and the tellers must not answer questions or volunteer information about the election except on matters of actual procedure.

If any member has reason to doubt the accuracy of the result, he can claim a recount of the votes.

Ballot papers should be as simple as possible. The names should be in alphabetical order and each scrutineer should be given a list with the names in the same order as on the ballot papers, with adequate space beside each name to record every vote received.

The names of those nominated as officers are also often included in the nominations for the committee as members may wish to elect them on to the committee even if they do not consider them suitable as officers.

THIRD ANNUAL GENERAL MEETING OF THE
G— YOUTH CLUB

BALLOT PAPER

President (or chairman) (1 vote)	*Hon. Secretary* (1 vote)	*Hon. Treasurer* (1 vote)
Mrs. W. Henry.	Miss Bird.	Mr. R.A. Thoms.
Mr. R. Williams.	Mrs. James.	

Committee
(not more than 5 votes)

Mrs. Alexandria.	Mr. R. Evelyn.	Mrs. James.
Miss Bird.	Mrs. W. Henry.	Sir W. Micosia.
Mr. Blair.	Mrs. Hope-Ever.	Mr. R. Williams.

Please put X against the names for which you wish to vote.
Incorrectly filled-in papers will be disqualified.
Do not sign your name on the ballot paper.

PROXY FORM

I am unable to attend the Annual General Meeting on 12th November (year),
Mr.
and appoint Mrs. .... as my Proxy.
Miss

Signed ....

Filling Vacancies and Co-opting

In many organisations, a certain latitude is given to the Executive committee regarding numbers. Many societies lay down a rule such as that *The Executive committee shall consist of twelve members, with power to add to their number up to a maximum of fifteen.* This means that twelve members must be elected at the annual general meeting, but if members wish, these vacancies can be left, to be filled or not at the discretion of the committee. This has the advantage of allowing the committee to include anyone of outstanding merit without waiting until the next annual general meeting. Even where this flexibility is not permitted, committees are almost invariably given the right to fill any vacancy which may occur through resignation.

When the committee wishes either to add a new member or to fill a vacancy, the nomination must be proposed, seconded and put to the vote at the next committee meeting. If elected, he assumes all the rights and voting power of a full committee member; but any such addition must be ratified at the next annual general meeting. For instance, if Mr. Smith is elected for three years in November and has to resign in the following March, whoever is appointed in his place does not automatically hold office for three years but only until the next annual general meeting, when his appointment must be confirmed by the members. Neither should anyone filling a vacancy be included amongst the members offering themselves for re-election en bloc.

Co-opting is not necessarily the same thing as filling a vacancy and there is some confusion on this point. While planning some unusual or specialised activity, the committee may feel the need for expert advice, so invite a specialist to join the committee temporarily for the purpose of advising on that particular subject. Such a person is often not concerned with the work of the society as a whole and is therefore not really competent to have a vote.

A co-opted member does not, in fact, usually have a vote, neither does his temporary appointment need confirming by the annual general meeting (unless it is proposed to make him a full committee member) as he will cease to attend the meetings when his specialised services are no longer required.

For instance, if an organisation was considering buying property it might co-opt a solicitor, or if erecting a building you might require the expert knowledge of a surveyor, builder and/or architect. Whether these co-opted members are entitled to vote depends on the Constitution. Co-opted members should clarify their position at their first meeting. Some Constitutions even state that co-opted members can only vote providing the motion does not change the Constitution or does not involve capital expenditure. All this should be explained to co-opted members at their first meeting.

Voting Power

Voting power is as follows, unless the rules of the organisation state otherwise:

Chairman. If elected direct to the office, he has a casting vote only. If elected first as a committee member, he is entitled to a member's vote in addition to the chairman's casting vote.

As a chairman should be impartial, he must use his power of voting with extreme circumspection, if at all, otherwise he lays himself open to a charge of bias.

Secretary and Treasurer. If elected direct to the offices, they have no vote; if made committee members first, they are entitled to vote.

Committee members: all have votes.

Co-opted members: may or may not have this privilege, depending upon the rules of the society.

Ex-Officio Members

In addition to the elected officers and members of a committee, there are certain others whose position in the society automatically carries with it the right of membership of a committee. These people are called ex-officio members, or members "by right of office".

Many organisations provide for this in the rules, but if nothing definite is stated, the following may be some guide:

1. The President of an organisation has the right to attend any meetings held by the organisation.

2. The chairman of the Executive committee as distinct from the President, is entitled to sit on any standing or sub-committee.

3. The Hon. Secretary of the Executive committee would be entitled to attend any gathering of secretaries of the society.

4. The Hon. Treasurer would be considered an ex-officio member of any committee dealing with the finances of the society.

5. The chairman of any committee which appoints a sub-committee is an ex-officio member of that sub-committee.

In practice, it is seldom that any officer takes advantage of this privilege, as the whole purpose of the committee system is to decentralise the work of running the society; but it does enable those ultimately responsible to the members to check up on the proper working of every section, should this be necessary. It is also sometimes extremely helpful to the committee concerned to have the advice of ex-officio members, who may be better informed on certain matters than they are themselves and therefore in a strong position to advise.

9

DEBATES AND DISCUSSIONS

DEBATES

Definition and Purpose

A debate is a verbal controversy between two or more people within well-defined rules. It seldom has an ulterior motive other than an academic interest in out-manoeuvring an opponent through reasoned argument, and is held for the pleasure and education of those taking part rather than for the purpose of propagating theories and ideas.

Rules

Subjects for debate should always be presented in the form of a motion and care is required in drafting to ensure absolute clarity. As explained elsewhere the wording must be in the positive or confusion may arise. For example, a motion *That capital punishment should not have been abolished* could be confusing, whereas *That capital punishment should be re-introduced* is quite clear: it is easier to speak for or against a positive than a negative motion.

Almost anything can be made the subject of a debate, but religious topics are better excluded, unless very expertly handled, as this subject may lead to bitter controversy and nearly always ends in trouble.

For a debate, at least two speakers and a chairman are necessary – one speaker in favour of the motion, the *Opener*, and the other against the motion, the *Opposer*. There can also be supporting speakers on both sides.

If the debate is run by a debating society, the rules of that society will lay down the procedure to be followed; if not, a few simple rules must be drawn up for the individual debate.

These should be as straightforward as possible, and the following may be some guide:

1. The subject for debate must be worded in the form of a motion.
2. The Opener and Opposer may each speak for a specific time, usually fifteen minutes.
3. Supporting speakers must not number more than two on each side, and their time must not be more than one-third of the time allotted to the principal speakers.
4. The debate will be thrown open for half an hour. Any member wishing to speak for or against the motion may do so for three minutes. No member may speak more than once.
5. The Opener may reply to his opponent for not more than five minutes. The Opposer has no right of reply.
6. Timing will be strictly observed.
7. All speakers must address the chair.
8. The chairman's ruling is final.

Procedure

Chairing a debate is not difficult, as there is unlikely to be any disturbance, and the chairman's chief function is to see that strict timing is kept and that no speaker wanders from the subject under debate. He should be quite ruthless on these two points. If a speaker is obviously going to exceed his allotted time, the chairman can ring the bell a minute or two before the time limit as a warning that he must now sum up; and if he still fails to finish on time, the chairman must stop him.

The chairman will open proceedings by reading the rules and introducing the speakers, as he would at a public meeting. He will then read the subject for debate and call upon the Opener to speak in favour of the motion.

The Opener will then deliver his speech, which should have been carefully prepared beforehand. He should marshal his facts clearly and concisely and avoid inaccurate or carelessly worded statements which will give an opening to his opponent.

When preparing such a speech, always analyse arguments and think out what counterblast can be brought against them. This uncovers the weak spots and enables them to be strengthened or changed, and also provides the speaker with answers to arguments his opponent may bring against him. When summing up, put the main points in the form of a challenge, such as "Does not my opponent agree that...". This causes him to spend some of his time in answering these points and may force him to change his tactics.

When the Opener has finished, the chairman will call upon the Opposer.

In preparing his speech, the Opposer should allow for time to be spent in answering the arguments of his opponent. He should therefore not plan for the full time at his disposal, but leave room to deal with the Opener's main points in addition to his own arguments. If he is quick-witted and an experienced debater, he will probably do very little definite planning of his speech but make himself thoroughly conversant with the subject and leave himself free to concentrate on demolishing his opponent's arguments rather than bring in too many fresh ones of his own; but this needs experience and a clear-thinking, flexible mind.

If there are supporting speakers on both sides, it is usual to call upon the supporter of the Opener to speak after the Opposer so that he has points to answer. Otherwise he can only amplify his leader's arguments, as he has not heard the other side. The supporter of the Opposer follows him, and so a clash of opinion is obtained all through the debate.

After both Openers and Opposers have finished, the chairman will throw the motion open for discussion. Speeches should be taken alternately for and against, if possible, to keep a proper balance, and it is usual to ask someone to speak in support of the motion first. Anyone wishing to do so will stand or raise his hand to catch the chairman's eye, but should not start to speak until requested, and must be careful not to exceed the allotted time.

Questions are not permitted in a debate (except to the chairman on a point of procedure) and there is no contact between the speakers and the audience as at a public meeting or in a discussion. Should a misapprehension arise as to what a speaker actually said, he may ask permission of the chairman to correct this, but must not regard this as an opportunity to elaborate his statement.

Care should be exercised to ensure that everyone who wishes to speak is given the opportunity, and no one should be allowed to speak a second time until all have had their turn. This last point is very important, particularly with beginners, who are not used to collecting their thoughts and marshalling facts quickly; without such a rule, they will be constantly jumping up to add afterthoughts.

As soon as the discussion period has expired, the chairman should refuse all further speeches and call upon the Opener to reply. When doing so, the Opener should confine himself to refuting his opponent's arguments and reiterating his own main points; he should not introduce any new matter.

Sometimes the Opposer is given a second opportunity, but it is not his by right and if this privilege is granted, he must speak again *before* the Opener, who always has the last word. Thus, the order should be:

1. Opener.
2. Opposer.
3. Opener's supporters, if any.
4. Opposer's supporters.
5. Speeches from audience.
6. Opposer, if granted the privilege.
7. Opener.

In either case, only the principal speakers reply; supporting speakers do not have this right.

When the Opener has replied, the chairman will put the motion to the vote, after which he will either put a vote of thanks from the chair or have one proposed and seconded formally as at a public meeting.

The winner will reply to this vote of thanks and the chairman will declare the debate closed.

DISCUSSIONS

Difference Between Debate and Discussion

There is some confusion between the purpose of a debate and a discussion, and people frequently state that they are taking part in a debate when it is actually a discussion.

A *debate* seeks to impart knowledge and convince through argument between selected speakers, and the chief function of the audience is to listen rather than to talk.

The purpose of a *discussion* is to extract ideas from the audience, whose function is to express those ideas in speech.

Debates are destructive as they present one-sided opinions and demolish reasoned arguments, whereas discussions are constructive and encourage the expression of opinion. The procedure therefore differs as follows:

In a public debate, the principal speakers are only concerned with answering each other and the period after their speeches is merely an opportunity for them to prepare their closing remarks while the audience discuss the subject under the guidance of the chairman. The audience need not and usually do not take any part in the discussion unless they wish to clarify previous points.

The Opener, in winding up, often refers to points raised in discussion and thanks supporters. He can then sum up the strong points of the proposition and demolish finally the objections, without introducing new material.

Discussion is very different. Speakers are there to present a reasoned case for or against the motion; and to help the audience reach a conclusion the chairman often sums up their points – which is never done in a debate – before inviting the co-operation of the audience and during the general discussion, the principal speakers answer questions.

Purpose of Discussion

Speech is necessary to clarify thought, as it is the natural method of crystallising nebulous emotions into practical ideas.

Discussions take us a step further and crystallise collective thought into combined action. They are the modern method of self-education, designed to meet the ever-increasing desire for a clearer grasp of current problems, so necessary to counter the isolation of individual thought which can easily lead to prejudiced and unbalanced judgment.

Their value is threefold: they ensure enlightened public opinion, which is essential to democratic society; they develop moral qualities such as friendliness, sincerity and tolerance; and they act as levellers by proving that *ideas* are not the prerogative of class or education.

Organisation

Everything possible should be done to create an atmosphere of physical relaxation and mental ease by having a cheerful, comfortable room and keeping reasonably informal. The chairman should make every effort to obtain a friendly feeling among those present, as ideas will flow more freely in a comfortable and pleasant atmosphere.

The subject for discussion need not necessarily be worded as a motion, though it is better if it takes this form as it is then easier to put to the vote at the end, if desired. A vote is usually taken either on the original or on one motion embodying the combined opinions of the members, which crystallises during discussion, but this is not the invariable rule as after a debate.

To enable the principal speakers to put up a good case, both should be given at least fifteen minutes; and anyone speaking in support should be allowed not more than one-third of this time. If there are supporting speakers, they should speak immediately after their leaders so that the case is built up and presented as a whole.

When each side has been presented, members of the audience can ask questions from any speaker as well as make observations of their own, and there is no need for such speeches to be alternately for and against, as in a debate, though the chairman must use his own discretion in this matter; as also on the question as to whether he allows more than one speech from any member. It is necessary to encourage the flow of ideas from the audience, but no one person should be permitted to dominate the discussion.

The general procedure is similar to that for a debate and the order will be:

Chairman's opening remarks

For { Speaker in favour of the motion – Opener.
Supporting speakers, if any.

Against { Speaker opposing the motion – Opposer.
Supporters, if any.

Summing up by chairman – optional.

Questions and speeches from audience.

Summing up by Opposer.

Summing up by Opener.

Vote put to meeting.

DISCUSSION GROUPS

Purpose of Discussion Groups

The aim of all discussion groups is to persuade members to think, listen and speak; and the order in which this is attempted varies to suit individual members, as some thinkers speak too rarely, while some speakers think too little and all of us absorb knowledge through listening. A good discussion-group leader can adjust the balance.

There are two schools of thought regarding discussion groups. Some organisations think that education should precede discussion and advocate a preliminary series of lectures, debates or quizzes as a means of imparting the necessary knowledge upon which to base argument.

Other organisations feel that the aim of a discussion group should be to extract ideas which can subsequently be buttressed by knowledge. This will be more readily absorbed when the need for it has been realised and interest stimulated by discussion. The latter method is more far-reaching, as many want to speak but few want to learn in the early stages; and it was certainly the method used by the Ancient Greeks, who were the pioneers of discussion groups.

Running discussions where group members are intelligent and well informed is comparatively easy, whereas it requires great skill, tact and patience to produce good results from the raw material of spontaneous ideas; so that the methods described here are intended for inexperienced leaders and informal groups in the experimental stage.

Organisation

In the early stages, the fewer the rules the better, as friendliness, tolerance and a keen desire to exchange ideas flourish best in a free atmosphere. Groups should be kept small – under twelve, if possible – so that each member feels that he must make his contribution. If a group is larger than this, its shy members tend to become spectators only.

The surroundings in which the group meets are very important. When starting a group, formality should be avoided. Have the room light and cheerful, with comfortable chairs, if possible, and arrange them in a circle (not rows), so that members' expressions can be seen. The whole interpretation of a remark can be altered by the speaker's expression, and this is lost if only the back of his head is visible.

The leader should not stand behind a table, as this isolates him and creates a wrong atmosphere. Informality is the keynote.

When choosing a subject for this type of group, word it carefully. For example, to ask beginners to discuss "Is space exploration necessary?" might have an overawing effect, whereas "Is there life in outer space?" would be more likely to produce opinions and could easily lead on to the discussion of space exploration.

Small informal groups usually have a leader only. Bigger groups sometimes divide the work between three officers, i.e. a chairman, to control the meeting; a secretary, to take the minutes; and a leader, who is thus left free to concentrate on the discussion.

The chairman's duties are confined to opening remarks; introducing the leaders and speakers, if any; ensuring that the rules, if there are any definite ones, are kept; timing speeches; taking a vote, should the group decide to record its opinions by means of a motion; and thanking speakers and the leader at the end. He should leave guidance of the discussion to the leader and should not try to direct or influence opinions unless asked to do so.

The secretary's duties are purely advisory and he can help both chairman and leader by keeping a record of speakers;

noting any information required at the next meeting; drafting motions and giving dictionary definitions of words if asked to do so by the leader in order to clarify the position, should two speakers interpret a word differently. Words are sharp tools which can be mis-handled with disastrous consequences.

Whether there is a chairman or not, the work of the leader remains the same.

Qualifications for a Leader

Great care should be taken in selecting the leader for a discussion group. The intellectual, highly qualified man (or woman) is not necessarily the most suitable person, as his mind tends to move at too high a level and he may find it difficult to tune in to the wave-length of the less-trained mind or to deal with a subject in its elementary stages.

It is essential that the leader should have a friendly and sympathetic disposition, able, at the outset, to create the right atmosphere of companionship and relaxation which are the best conditions to induce the flow of ideas. He must be tactful and patient and avoid any hint of sarcasm or cynicism, as these will completely paralyse nervous members. He must be able to restrain his own opinions and keep his temper under provocation.

Starting a Group

When starting a discussion group for teenagers it is usually inadvisable to have a speaker at first, as members are not yet able to undertake this themselves and the presence of an outsider may result in a giggling, tongue-tied group.

It is better for the leader to open with a short informal talk on the subject, which should be light and within the range of all. A personal anecdote or funny story makes the best type of approach, followed by a few words on the lines already given. The leader can then ask if anyone has had a similar experience or holds the same opinions. If no response is forthcoming, he can call upon someone by name. The technique with this type of group is to drop the seed of an idea, then to extract the resultant growth of an opinion, however tentative and ill-formed, so encouraging self-expression and further thought.

After one or two such meetings, when the members have become more or less at ease, a speaker can be introduced, perhaps as "a friend of mine who knows a bit about this subject". When choosing this first outside speaker, care should be taken to select the right personality, as anyone who lacks a sense of humour or dominates the meeting may undo the good work of the leader in creating an easy atmosphere.

As soon as possible, the members can be encouraged to act as speakers themselves, and the group built up in this way as it widens its range and outlook. If the correct attitude has been inculcated from the outset, the friendly atmosphere will continue, even after the discussions have adopted the more formal procedure necessary to the running of a larger group.

Perhaps one of the main difficulties with which the leader of this type of group has to contend is the varying mental development shown by the members. The giggler, the exhibitionist, the inarticulate, the over-earnest or the precocious, even the vicious type will be encountered; and to recognise, understand and handle each effectively, while keeping the balance true, requires considerable ability and experience. Running such a group is not easy and carries a very real responsibility, but it can play an immense part in developing the minds and characters of the members and is well worth the effort.

Advanced Groups

Duties of a Leader. The five main duties of a leader are:

1. Preliminary preparation.
2. Opening discussion.
3. Guiding and co-ordinating ideas.
4. Summing up.
5. Planning future work.

Of these duties, the first is the most important and onerous, as the success of the meeting largely depends upon the initial planning done by the leader.

Preliminary preparation includes a survey of the subject, collecting and planning material, studying the members, selecting suitable openings and giving some thought to a possible follow-up.

(a) Collecting Material. The enthusiasm of the leader is a vital factor in stimulating discussion and this can best be generated by examining his own feelings about the subject in hand.

The leader's own ideas should be written out very briefly, pruned, checked and the gaps filled up. A leader is not expected to be an expert, but his opinion will frequently be asked and he needs a background of general knowledge if he is to maintain his authority.

The more factual the subject, the more knowledge is required and he should therefore be in a position to tell members where it can be obtained if he cannot supply it himself. Where funds are available, many groups authorise their leaders to purchase pamphlets, maps or visual aids, and a dictionary is always useful.

Light subjects are recommended to begin with and the leader should draw on his stock of humour. He will find it helpful to put down six or more obvious points and to concentrate on an amusing or interesting illustration for each, with which he can amplify the discussion and keep it on a light note. When any of these points arise, he can, if desirable, flatter the speaker and raise a laugh by adding his own illustration; and if the discussion flags, he can use his points as pegs on which members may hang their words: but it is better for him to wait for the points to emerge naturally – as they probably will; if obvious, they are common property.

(b) Planning. Having collected his material, the leader should plan the possible development of the discussion by grouping ideas. Such a plan must be kept in reserve, as the leader's job is to guide the discussion down the path selected by the members and not to determine it himself; but the trend of ideas can usually be foreseen, if the right lead is given in the initial stages. Planned coherency will result.

After this he can group ideas under three or four main headings, which will act as the cornerstones in building up the discussion. He will find that this is the most satisfactory way of preventing rambling speeches which kill enthusiasm as they lead to a feeling of frustration rather than of achievement. He can allocate so much time to each group of ideas, and ask members merely to signify support for arguments already developed, instead of repeating them, as this will allow time for fresh ideas.

When the ideas have been grouped, the leader should arrange them in logical order to ensure continuity, and he should prepare a link sentence which he can introduce after summing up in order to switch ideas to another level.

Once the leader has thoroughly absorbed his plan, he will only require a card with main headings, sub-headings and link sentences for reference, as he is not a lecturer and should not need copious notes.

(c) Studying Members. A leader should know the members of his group personally, if this is possible, and also something of their backgrounds, as experiences colour knowledge and opinions, and an understanding of this will enable him to anticipate the trend of their remarks to a surprising extent. He will know where to turn for humour, tact or expert knowledge and can allocate suitable speakers for each group of ideas, if he wishes. Care must be taken, however, to include newcomers and to give them priority over the old hands at their first attempt.

(d) Suitable Openings. The leader's fourth and last preliminary duty is to decide the best way to initiate discussion. He can choose any of the following methods and should vary his approach:

(i) A ten minute talk by himself, outlining the subject and suggesting three or four main headings for discussion. If he thinks this method betrays obvious planning and savours of "direction", he can conclude by saying that the questions arise logically and the group should try to answer them.

(ii) Selecting members to make opening speeches is a useful beginning. Four members might be asked to submit a point of interest on which they are prepared to speak. It is often desirable to arrange a previous meeting with these speakers, to co-ordinate ideas and avoid overlapping. Each speech should be followed by discussion limited to the main ideas expounded. By making one speech the pivot of argument for a certain time, the field of discussion is limited, whereas if each speaker ranges over too wide a field of ideas, it becomes unwieldy. Four speakers, given five minutes each, followed by fifteen minutes' discussion on each talk and five minutes for the leader's summing up, is an orderly pattern for a meeting of one and a half hours.

(iii) A ten minute talk by an expert, followed by ten minutes of questions and answers before the subject is thrown open to discussion, is a well-known practice. The danger is that the expert often controls the leader, and the time allowed is short, so that little time may be left for discussion. A better plan is to ask the expert to suggest half a dozen points for discussion and to arrange a meeting with him again later, at which the conclusions of the group will be submitted for his consideration.

Leader's Work at the Meeting. This consists in guiding the discussion, clarifying and recording opinions, summing up at intervals, drafting a motion if desired, and suggesting future activities.

Recording opinions is very difficult and recording sheets are helpful. If the leader is starting each section of the discussion himself with an initial question covering the points to be discussed, and the subject chosen is "Is space exploration necessary?", the recording sheets might be as follows:

Subject: "Is space exploration necessary?"
Groups of ideas: 1. Personal views.
2. Achievements.
3. International relationships.
4. Natural resources.

1. *Personal Views.* Initial question: Do you think space exploration is an inevitable step forward in man's progress?

(See table overleaf)

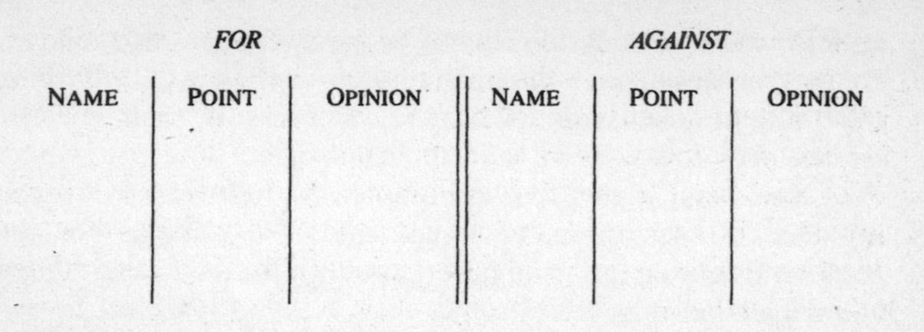

FOR			*AGAINST*		
NAME	POINT	OPINION	NAME	POINT	OPINION

Summing up.

Majority view.....

Minority view.....

Information required.

Separate recording sheets are required for each section.

Suggested initial questions for the other three points might be:

2. *Achievements.* What has the space programme achieved so far? Do its achievements justify its existence?

3. *International relationships.* Do you think space exploration might provide a common aim for the world and so promote unity?

4. *Natural resources.* Natural resources on earth may one day be exhausted, does this make the exploration of space essential?

Summing up. This must be clear cut and in no sense evasive, even if it means agreeing to disagree.

Final summing up is merely the co-ordination of the majority view for recording purposes and can be in the form of a motion.

Information Required. Preliminary discussion often discloses the need for further information, which the leader should note and, if the subject is too big for one evening, a series of discussions might be suggested, to deal with various aspects.

Teaching Through Discussion

This form of Discussion Group has also proved a highly

satisfactory way of giving instruction to small groups.

The conditions should be the same as for any discussion group – informality and comfort, and it is advisable to have not more than six or eight in the group.

In this case the leader is, of course, knowledgeable on the subject to be discussed, and his purpose is to find out, through questions, what members of the group know, or think, on the subject, and then either to correct or supplement their ideas. This has the merit of ensuring that there are no "gaps" left in their minds, and also discloses misapprehensions and prejudices which do not so readily come to light in the ordinary method of teaching through lecturing.

The teacher requires careful preparation of the subject to be dealt with, and should make a series of notes so that he can ensure that the discussion does not roam too far from the point. The technique here is to start by asking a question and drawing out the knowledge of the group members *before* imparting knowledge. In this way the interest of the group is maintained throughout. Care must be taken to ensure that every member is brought in.

INDEX

Companion volume in the same series

THE HON. TREASURER

A book for the inexperienced treasurer of a voluntary organisation filled with practical guidance on doing the job well.

Written by a chartered accountant with experience of the roles of both Hon. Treasurer and Hon. Auditor, it goes through keeping the basic records and on to financial controls, planning, preparing the final accounts and facing the audit.

Having given support and advice to a number of treasurers throughout the years, Roderick Boucher has used his experience of the problems that arise, and the areas that confuse, to write this book which will be a constant source of reference and reassurance to anyone new to the role of Hon. Treasurer.

Uniform with this book

In the same series

YOUR VOICE
How to Enrich it, and Develop it for Speaking, Acting and Everyday Conversation

A simple but valuable guide for those who want to polish and improve their most potent means of communication: the voice. Become aware of the parts of your body which need to work to peak performance for clear, dynamic and persuasive speech. Be guided through the use of crisp consonants and well shaped vowels. Learn expressiveness, projection, confidence and relaxation.

PRESENTATIONS
The Right Way To Make Effective Presentations

J Stuart Williams has given hundreds of presentations all over the world, for sales, technical and training purposes. He'll help you to prepare thoroughly, speak with confidence, emphasise the key points with visual aids and control your audience so that you always give an *effective* presentation.

Uniform with this book

In the same series

BOOK-KEEPING THE RIGHT WAY

This book is for the self-employed, the small businessman and for the treasurer of any club or voluntary organisation. It explains the principles of correct book-keeping simply and in a logical sequence. It is equally useful for people keeping manual records and for those who will be keeping accounts on a computer.

THE RIGHT WAY TO WRITE REPORTS

A good report summarises the facts clearly, draws the correct conclusions, and gives the right recommendations for future action. With Steve Gravett's help *you* will be able to compile reports which are clear, succinct, accurate, fair and well-written.

HANDLING PUBLICITY THE RIGHT WAY

Publicity is the key to selling your product or promoting your cause. Here journalist and media training consultant John Venables shows how it can be used to best effect. He'll give you the skills and knowledge you need to attract public attention if you want to be in the limelight – and how to cope if you don't!

Uniform with this book

RIGHT WAY
PUBLISHING POLICY

HOW WE SELECT TITLES

RIGHT WAY consider carefully every deserving manuscript. Where an author is an authority on his subject but an inexperienced writer, we provide first-class editorial help. The standards we set make sure that every **RIGHT WAY** book is practical, easy to understand, concise, informative and delightful to read. Our specialist artists are skilled at creating simple illustrations which augment the text wherever necessary.

CONSISTENT QUALITY

At every reprint our books are updated where appropriate, giving our authors the opportunity to include new information.

FAST DELIVERY

We sell **RIGHT WAY** books to the best bookshops throughout the world. It may be that your bookseller has run out of stock of a particular title. If so, he can order more from us at any time – we have a fine reputation for ''same day'' despatch, and we supply any order, however small (even a single copy), to any bookseller who has an account with us. We prefer you to buy from your bookseller, as this reminds him of the strong underlying public demand for **RIGHT WAY** books. Readers who live in remote places, or who are house-bound, or whose local bookseller is uncooperative, can order direct from us by post.

FREE

If you would like an up-to-date list of all **RIGHT WAY** titles currently available, please send a stamped self-addressed envelope to
ELLIOT RIGHT WAY BOOKS, BRIGHTON ROAD,
LOWER KINGSWOOD, TADWORTH, SURREY, KT20 6TD, U.K.
or visit our web site at www.right-way.co.uk